Crosscurrents / MODERN CRITIQUES

Harry T. Moore, *General Editor*

Age of the Modern
And Other Literary Essays

Harry T. Moore

SOUTHERN ILLINOIS UNIVERSITY PRESS
Carbondale and Edwardsville

FEFFER & SIMONS, INC.
London and Amsterdam

IN MEMORY OF

Richard Rees

friend, editor, author, painter

Contents

Introduction

This Introduction consists of notes and comments on the writings which appear in this volume. Most readers will want to skip this section and read the book for its own sake. I hope, however, since the subtitle promised essays, that no one will be too shocked to find the volume opening with a poem. This might be called an assay in the now obsolete meaning of that word: an attempt (also an essay).

When Sir Richard Rees and John Middleton Murry printed "Psalm of Los Angeles" in the March 1934 issue of the *Adelphi*, it was my first "professional" appearance in print after a number of sports articles written some years before for the *Panama American*. "Psalm of Los Angeles" indicates in several passages a dawning social consciousness of which its author was unaware when he wrote it in 1933, as today he is unaware of the source of the terror motif: perhaps a young man groping toward the symbolistic? The poem is somewhat Eliotic in tone, possibly because it was written soon after T. S. Eliot had publicly read *The Waste Land* in, of all places, Los Angeles. A discussion of Eliot's reading of his own verse occurs later in this book, in the "Poetry on Records" section.

From "Psalm of Los Angeles" to "Anatomy of Chicago" is quite a leap. The latter is a 1937 *New Republic* review of Meyer Levin's *The Old Bunch*, which the Viking Press thought durable enough to reissue in the 1960s.

Before I went into war service, Malcolm Cowley often

sent books for review in the *New Republic*. The one here (from 1939) called "Dorothy Richardson's Journey" dealt with her *Pilgrimage*, which then consisted of a dozen novels in four volumes. A thirteenth and posthumous volume appeared a few years ago, but my original judgments seem to me to stand up well enough across the years, so here they are. And certainly such reviews, on which a writer spends a great deal of effort, may legitimately be called essays.

"The Great Unread (D. H. Lawrence in 1940)" was a signed *Saturday Review of Literature* (as it was then) editorial noting the tenth anniversary of Lawrence's death. The essay is reprinted here partly in answer to an accusation that its author had climbed onto the Lawrence bandwagon rather late. But in 1940 there was no bandwagon to climb onto. As William White's 1950 book, *D. H. Lawrence: A Checklist*, shows—and Mr. White points up the fact in his preface—Lawrence's reputation, which had never been more than a minority one—began sinking in 1934 and reached its lowest point by 1942.

Any reader who isn't interested in bibliography or literary controversy should ignore the paragraph now in process, for it is intended only to set the Lawrence-criticism record straight. In the *Nation* of October 23, 1936, my review of *Phoenix: The Posthumous Papers of D. H. Lawrence* found in that volume "enough of general interest and enough of Lawrence at his best to make this an influential book." Few other American critics at that midpoint of the Depression discovered any virtues in *Phoenix*, and in the *New Yorker* Clifton Fadiman sneered at it as "dated." But *Phoenix* has risen from its ashes, and in its recent editions has become indeed an influential book. In the April 1937 number of *Reading and Collecting: A Monthly Review of Rare and Recent Books*, my article "Another Side of D. H. Lawrence" stated that he was one of the first men to understand the issues of our time "for their true values." My December 28, 1938 *New Republic* review, "The Status of D. H. Lawrence," defended him from Hugh Kingsmill's disparaging and now forgotten biography and said that Lawrence's work provided "one of the great reading experiences of our time." My review of William York Tindall's *D. H. Lawrence and*

Susan His Cow in the *Saturday Review of Literature* for October 28, 1939 again defended Lawrence, though I admired Mr. Tindall's scholarship; he thought the review fair minded, and we became good friends. (Yes, Virginia, it is possible for people to be on opposite sides in critical matters without exhibiting bad manners.)

That last paragraph provides a somewhat pedagogical background to "The Great Unread (D. H. Lawrence in 1940)," but it does set the Lawrence-scholarship record straight. I have written much about Lawrence since then and have edited or coedited several volumes of his writings, which critics and other readers began to appreciate by the early 1950s. Before then there were few favorable references to Lawrence, especially in America, or he was simply ignored. It is impossible for me to refrain from quoting the conclusion of "The Great Unread (D. H. Lawrence in 1940)," which prophesied that "his work will be called back, as Melville's was, among the living." I think that most of the statements in that little essay will stand today, and it certainly shows that its author didn't capitalize on Lawrence after he became "an established classic."

A minor figure comes next in this book: Upton Sinclair. Here are two discussions, from issues of the *Saturday Review of Literature* in 1940 and '41, of the first two novels in Sinclair's sequence of books about Lanny Budd. When *World's End* appeared, at an exciting moment in history, my review predicted that interest in the recently neglected Sinclair would be reawakened, as it was. Yet, despite its breath-catching quality, the book had flaws, and these had to be noted. The flaws were even more evident in the next volume, *Between Two Worlds*, and I told the *Saturday Review of Literature* I didn't want to review any more books in the series, which continued with great success, though I have been unable to plough through any of the later volumes. Yet Sinclair wasn't altogether a negligible writer; Bernard Shaw praised him highly, and D. H. Lawrence, whose critical allegiance was not easily won, said he had read Sinclair's novel *Oil!* "with keen interest," regarding it "as a big splendid picture of actual life."

"Poetry on Records" offers a different kind of discussion,

taken from two reviews from the section of that name appearing in *Poetry: A Magazine of Verse* both before and after the Second World War, first under the editorship of George Dillon and later under that of Karl Shapiro. There were also spoken-poetry articles for *Theatre Arts* ("Shakespeare on Records"), Klaus Mann's *Decision*, and one of the *New Directions* annuals. I was pioneering in the field and creating a special career, but became so busy writing various books during the 1950s that all the listening to and playing and replaying of speaking records became a burden, and I retired to other types of writing.

One of these is represented by "An Ernest Hemingwaiad," which Stephen Spender published in *Encounter* in 1958. Although cast in the form of a poem, this "Hemingwaiad" contains as many critical statements as an essay of equal length. The use of the so-called heroic couplet is of course in the tradition of satire, and there was implied kidding in the use of anything, in the Hemingway context, called heroic. The "Hemingwaiad" was entirely impersonal. When it came out, an American author wrote to say it was good that people were aware that I didn't know Hemingway; the statement wasn't a suggestion that Hemingway might beat me up, but rather an intimation that it sounded like a product of personal malice which only a dear friend would turn out—but I never met, wrote to, or even saw Hemingway. His end in 1961 was a sad one, but now that he's been dead for some nine years this little bite at his career can do him no harm.

We have Lawrence again with the 1959 review of *Lady Chatterley's Lover* from the *New York Times Book Review*. My review annoyed the executors of the Lawrence Estate, who said they hadn't authorized the Grove Press publication, but I explained that I hadn't known this and had simply reviewed the book when Francis Brown sent it. The review represents my attitude, not shared by all commentators on Lawrence, to the effect that *Lady Chatterley* is an important book, though not Lawrence's finest. I had dealt with this novel in *The Life and Works of D. H. Lawrence* (1951) and in *The Intelligent Heart: The Story of D. H.*

Lawrence (1955), as well as in the introduction to the collection of Lawrence's *Essays on Sex, Literature and Censorship* (1953). And then in 1962 there was the fairly long afterword to the New American Library's Signet edition (authorized!) of *Lady Chatterley's Lover*. But the *Times* review included here contains much that is essential in my continuing judgment of the book, and it makes some special points, such as the rather inverse ancestry of Constance Chatterley in the persons of Emma Bovary and Anna Karenina.

Among several reviews of Kay Boyle (*New York Times, Saturday Review*, etc.), perhaps the most representative is that of *Generation Without Farewell*, which Robie Macauley sent me for discussion in the *Kenyon Review* in 1960. Kay Boyle's entire career up to that point is surveyed and, as a pleasant bracketing indicates, the Crosscurrents/ Modern Fiction series of the Southern Illinois University Press has reprinted Kay Boyle's two earliest novels, *Plagued by the Nightingale* and *Year Before Last*. (These are special textual editions prepared by Matthew J. Bruccoli.)

John Dos Passos is an extremely different kind of novelist from Kay Boyle, yet because both of them brought out their first complete books in the 1920s they did their early writing in a time of craftsmanship, when most serious novelists didn't turn out the slovenly prose of today, and when they demonstrated a knowledge of technique. Dos Passos is of course best known for his *U. S. A.* trilogy. He followed this with his *District of Columbia* trilogy, which embodied the change in his attitude; from a liberal-left position he swung to the right. Critics felt that his political switch was accompanied by an almost complete loss of talent. But as one who regards himself a seasoned liberal, I could greet *Midcentury*, in a 1961 front-page review in the *New York Times Book Review*, as something of a comeback. It seemed to me that John Dos Passos, whose early works I had admired, had by 1961 become less reactionary. A longtime champion of individualism, he had realized that a new kind of authoritarianism in big business was killing individualism; *Midcentury* is the first novel by an important writer which makes use of some of the postwar sociological changes in America, as explored by David Riesman and other social scientists. All this is suggested in the review; most other commentators seemed unable to find any improvement in the author of the *District of Columbia* trilogy.

"Henry Miller: From under the Counter to Front Shelf" first appeared in the *New York Times Book Review* in 1961, when the Grove Press boldly published a book whose Paris edition Americans had been smuggling into this country since before the Second World War. In defying censorship, the Grove Press was extensively successful, as with *Lady Chatterley's Lover*, in court battles over the book. This review of *Tropic of Cancer* is, among other things, a survey of Henry Miller's entire career.

The short essay "The Language of Fiction" was one of the "Speaking of Books" features in the *New York Times Book Review* in 1962. Although other examples of such "language" could be given in the instances of authors merely cited, the essay has been left in its original compressed form. Elsewhere in this volume the reader will find examples of prose by other imaginative writers, including D. H. Lawrence and Virginia Woolf.

The longer essays on William Dean Howells' *The Rise of Silas Lapham* and on Ivan Aleksandrovitch Goncharov's *Oblomov* need no introductory comment; they were written, respectively, as an afterword and a foreword to the Signet Classics editions of those novels. I wish there were space for my Signet Classics foreword to H. G. Wells's *Tono-Bungay*.

To follow a discussion of the troubles of Goncharov with "Comment on Leavis" is one of those amusing ironies that chronological arrangement sometimes causes. Ordinarily one wouldn't have reprinted this acid "Comment," originally a letter in the *Sewanee Review* in 1963, but a certain circumstance has dictated its inclusion here.

Once again, the reader who is not interested in literary controversy is warned away from the paragraphs immediately following. He can turn to the "Comment" itself, which is shorter than this commentary on it will be.

An earlier passage of this Introduction established my credentials as an ardent advocate of Lawrence, going as far back, in print, as the middle 1930s—though the advocacy began long before then, and I was one of the first Lawrence students to visit that part of the Midlands which is now the Lawrence Country. Anyhow, the public advocacy began long before Lawrence had a bandwagon to climb onto. But, in the *Sewanee Review* of Winter 1963, F. R. Leavis, in a purported review of my two-volume edition of *The Collected Letters of D. H. Lawrence*, wrote: "Professor Moore takes over Lawrence as an established classic on whom he has been able to consolidate his own position as an 'authority' with immediate academic credit and munificent institutional support."

That the first part of this sentence is untrue has been demonstrated earlier in this Introduction. But one wonders why Dr. Leavis is compelled to make such statements—though of course the psychological roots of the statement are visible in the dirty soil. As for the last part of the sentence, following the word *classic*, an utterance of that kind is usually called unprofessional in a community dedicated to the dignity of learning (including the learning of decent conduct). In certain other quarters, the last part of that sentence would be called dirty pool. Of course no one should be surprised to find Dr. Leavis indulging in insults. Looking over his career, one can observe that he began to be more splenetic and frantic about twelve or fifteen years ago, when he was ingloriously defeated in his attempt to be elected Professor of Poetry at Oxford, which his sycophants ironically felt was his due because the genuinely human, humane, and humanistic Matthew Arnold once held the position, and they consider him, at the very least, another Arnold. One of his freest indulgences in insult was in 1969, in a lecture on " 'English'—Unrest and Continuity," which was printed in the (London) *Times Literary Supplement*. Several of the people who had been splattered protested in later issues of the *TLS*, among them David Daiches, who wrote, "I have always tried to keep controversy on literary matters on a level of courteous and reasonable discourse, but it really is hard to remain unruffled after Dr. Leavis' gratuitous assault on myself," which Dr. Daiches characterized as the result of "hysteria," then concluded: "I must say that Dr. Leavis' own behavior is no testimony to the humanizing effects of the discriminating study of literature."

In 1970, another of the Leavis victims, Lord Annan, began a leading article in the *TLS* by saying, "Controversy is a dispiriting pastime, and controversy with Dr. Leavis is degrading. Degrading because you find his personal animosity puts such a strain on your temper and humor that to your horror you find yourself on the point of replying in his own tone of voice." Lord Annan resists the temptation and, at the end of a long essay full of reasoned argument, he quite properly and with marvelously good manners characterizes the argument-by-insult man: "No one can doubt the strength of Dr. Leavis' conviction that he is one of the few guardians of 'life,' 'creativity,' and 'health.' But can one accept such a claim from a man who declares that he is open to conviction yet habitually uses the language of intimidation to all who differ from his views; who alludes to evidence and doesn't give it; who speaks for the need of life and health in order to fortify his quasi-religious position but seems to be eaten up by rancor and hatred of life?"

These are representative remarks. Back in 1962 one could go along with a statement by Edmund Wilson which suggested that Leavis wasn't really worth reading. Wilson, a critic of indisputable stature (whatever his occasional mistakes), a versatile master of both exposition and analysis, said he had heard that "parts of [Leavis's] books are brilliant. But I haven't read those books, and when I have read him, he was always railing against somebody. He's the kind of dogmatic person who inevitably antagonizes me. I can't understand making a life-or-death issue out of one's preference for this or that writer." This was a cool, civilized statement, made in the year in which William Heinemann, Ltd., and the Viking Press brought out my edition of Lawrence's *Letters*.

The reviews were mostly good, except from one Leavisite,

though many of the commentators complained because the *Letters* were *Collected* rather than *Complete*; but the publishers had limited the editor to two volumes. As the reader already knows, Dr. Leavis wrote a "review" of them for the *Southern Review*; but it ignored Lawrence's *Letters* almost entirely and attacked the editor, in the process assembling a massive array of trivialities.

The *Sewanee Review* agreed to print a riposte, but allowed such little space for it that there was no chance to answer Dr. Leavis point by point; the comment had to be concise and suggestive. The result is printed in this book. The mail which came in after it appeared indicated that it had struck the right note: one report even said that the letter had caused some screaming and stamping across the sea. The author of a fine book on Lawrence wrote to say that the Leavis piece *couldn't* be left unanswered; the writer said he'd wondered, however, just *how* it could be answered, and he felt that the riposte was exactly right. Another author of a first-rate study of Lawrence liked most of the letter, but regretted that at the end it had to stoop to quoting William Gerhardi (who has since somehow become Gerhardie). I explained to this correspondent that Gerhardie had been quoted with extreme deliberateness, out of apprehension that the *Sewanee Review* might not print the letter if it applied an appropriate clinical term. But it was safe to quote William Gerhardie, who had used an applicable phrase in the venerably secure pages of the *Spectator* after Leavis's ferocious onslaught against C. P. Snow.

After the *Sewanee Review* letter, I was willing to retire from the fray and take a somewhat detached Edmund-Wilsonian attitude. But in 1967 Dr. Leavis reprinted his "review" of the Lawrence *Letters* in a volume of his own writings. The slur against my professional standing was repeated. (The American Association of University Professors has advised members of the academic community to use "appropriate restraint" in public utterances, and although the suggestion probably has a socio-political reference, it could also apply to professorial manners.) Further, the accusation that I had capitalized on Lawrence after he had become "an established classic" was also repeated. I had denied this and had referred to those contributions to journals which praised Lawrence when his reputation was at its lowest. Perhaps Dr. Leavis didn't have time to hunt up the references, though all the items are registered in William White's 1950 *Checklist*. But Dr. Leavis simply is not interested in the truth. I had challenged the accuracy of his statement, and he repeated that statement, which had by then become a lie.

With that out of the way, we can take up the subject of Theodore Dreiser and the appropriateness (or lack of it) of W. A. Swanberg as his biographer. Admittedly, Dreiser as an author doesn't have the stature of a Herman Melville or a Henry James; yet he ranks high among the novelists of his own time. It is too early to determine his exact standing among his contemporaries, yet it is safe to say that his novels, along with Willa Cather's and Edith Wharton's, stand out as the finest produced in America during the first twenty years of this century. Further, Dreiser's *An American Tragedy* holds its own against most American novels of the 1920s. The review reprinted here defends big, clumsy Dreiser against W. A. Swanberg, who is a conscientiously thorough biographer, excellent when he deals with such men as William Randolph Hearst; but an imaginative writer needs as his biographer someone who is an expert in literature rather than social history. Incidentally, this review is one of several written for the *Chicago Tribune*, a paper which often irritated me during a long residence in what it called "Chicagoland." It was a surprise to find a British liberal-left writer, while teaching in America before his return to Great Britain, writing reviews for the *Tribune*, with whose policies he certainly disagreed. He explained that he wrote as he pleased, and that the literary section had no politics, as I discovered when the *Tribune*'s literary editor, Robert Cromie, invited me to write reviews for him.

"Simenon's Artist-Saint of the rue Mouffetard," one of a number of contributions to the *Saturday Review* since Rochelle Girson became book-review editor, appeared in a 1965 issue. Admittedly, Georges Simenon isn't a "great" writer, but he is often a pleasant one. I've written reviews of more important books for the *Saturday Review*—in that same year of 1965, the Yeats centennial, I discussed seven of the new volumes about him, and now in June 1970 I've reviewed two more Yeats items—but the Simenon review is included here largely because of its Parisian *ambiance*. The old marketplace of Paris, Les Halles, in the first arrondissement, which plays so important a part in the Simenon novel, no longer exists; these days, the taxi driver taking you into the city from Orly airport points out the buildings of the huge new marketplace that is out in the country. And the rue Mouffetard, where Simenon's "little saint" grows up, is now threatened by new-style real-estate developments. An American and a group of Frenchmen are trying, according to *Publishers' Weekly* of June 8, 1970, to persuade the Ministry of Culture to prevent the construction of a high-rise apartment building above La Mouffe, "the rue Mouffetard market and housing site in which Hemingway wrote in the 1920s, over a room in which the poet Verlaine died, and which he described so vividly in *A Moveable Feast*." Ralph Feigelson, the concerned American, told the *New York Times*, "It is not just the stones of the houses that we want to preserve. We want to keep the contours of the little streets, the shape of the skyline, the way people live—the whole environment." It's really rather a scroungy district, though it is picturesque as well as historical. If Simenon's novel captures its atmosphere, perhaps this review of the book will reflect at least a little of it.

The next piece, "Some Notes on John Steinbeck's Later Works," formed the 1968 epilogue to the second edition of my book *The Novels of John Steinbeck*, first published in 1939, when it came out on the same day as Steinbeck's *The Grapes of Wrath*. My critical study (not really "critical" enough!) included a discussion of that novel because the late Benedict Abramson, the Chicago bookseller, had obtained galley proofs in advance of publication and kindly lent these to me. My review of earlier Steinbeck books in the *New Republic* had been enthusiastic, but by 1939 disillusion was setting in, to be increased in 1942, when *The Moon is Down* was published; fakery had taken over. In the *New Republic* in 1956 and in *American Literature* the following year, my reviews of books by and about Steinbeck manifested a continuing disappointment with his work. These reviews are the basis of the epilogue to the second edition of *The Novels of John Steinbeck*, which came out in 1968, reproducing even the map of "the Steinbeck Country," but containing new material in its foreword and epilogue. (Several years before, the book had been honored when a New York bookseller brought it out in a "pirated" edition, which he was forced to withdraw.) The new epilogue is reprinted here because it has the possibility of being somewhat corrective. If there is one school of criticism today that features snarled insults (reflecting unhappy childhoods?), there is another, of an altogether different kind, that cheerfully overrates an author or a book, as when Steinbeck is compared to Shakespeare, Dante, or Rabelais. This is safe to do only with an indisputably major figure. And, as this epilogue points out, none of the leading American critics have accepted Steinbeck as a first-rate writer.

Admittedly, it is sometimes dangerous to make too-assured negative judgments about an author, even though the seemingly best critics are in agreement on the point. For posterity has a peculiar way of dealing with these matters, and long after the critics and the professors have had their say, Dr. Johnson's "Common Reader" makes the final determination. Still, one can't be a serious reader in one's own time without setting up some standards. In the case of Ernest Hemingway, opinion as to the ultimate value of his work is divided. As the "Hemingwaiad" shows, the present writer belongs to the school which thinks Hemingway's earliest work is his best, a point brought out again in the next piece in this book, a review of Carlos Baker's 1969 biography of Hemingway. This is one of a number of reviews written for Van Allen Bradley of the *Chicago Daily News*, who besides being an editor and critic is an expert on rare books. This Hemingway review is a bit rough on Carlos Baker, whom I like and admire, but his book has been so hugely successful that he can stand a few little bumps. Like the review of W. A. Swanberg's biography of Dreiser—and one which occurs later, dealing with Zelda Fitzgerald—this discussion of Hemingway raises some issues about the writing of literary biographies.

Across the years I've reviewed several books by John O'Hara for the *New York Times Book Review*, but for inclusion here have selected a brief later (1969) discussion, from the *Chicago Daily News*, of the last of his novels which appeared in print before his death: *Lovey Childs*. Although this is a fairly short novel, without the bulk of *A Rage to Live* or *From the Terrace*—those popular successes which to me seem artistic failures—it reveals the flaws in O'Hara as a novelist, his inability to make various parts join, especially when he tries to range across time. O'Hara was a notable observer and recorder of manners, but he did his finest work in the short story, in which he usually had to deal only with a single situation.

Because the "Age of the Modern" piece gives this book its title, we had considered putting this essay at the beginning. It was written several years ago, but revised in 1970. I'll let it speak for itself, but will make one explanation in regard to it: I am not educated in the technique of music, though I have listened to good music for many years and play it daily on the phonograph (and just at this moment the Valkyries are whooping it up); my remarks about musical technique in this title-essay are based on what I have read or heard spoken; one friend who was kind enough to give me some explanations has been thanked privately but will not be mentioned here lest he be blamed for any blunders the essay might contain in its discussion of music.

Next we come to Thomas Wolfe, who raged across space and time and only now and then was truly effective. My enthusiastic review of his second novel, *Of Time and the River*, in the *Adelphi* in 1935 doesn't measure my present attitude toward him. One soon finds, in teaching Wolfe in American-novel courses, that the best text to use is *The Short Novels of Thomas Wolfe*, consisting of five novellas. When Wolfe diffused some of this material through his long novels, it lost its force. "A Portrait of Bascom Hawke," for instance, is in its original form a story of some power, with a vivid central character; but when this novella is fragmented into parts in *Of Time and the River,* it is spoiled.

These comments set the background for the discussion of Wolfe's *Notebooks,* which was the leading review in a 1970 issue of the *Saturday Review.* It shows a certain sympathy with the changes of attitude Wolfe was undergoing toward the end of his life. The piece needs no further comment.

Zelda, Nancy Milford's biography of Mrs. F. Scott Fitzgerald, was the front-page review in the June 14, 1970 *New York Times Book Review.* It needs no explanation, but I'd like to admit a fondness for Scott Fitzgerald's novels, especially *Tender is the Night.* As indicated in the preface to Richard Lehan's fine study of Fitzgerald in the Crosscurrents/Modern Critiques series, I consider that novel one of the few which in our time are authentically tragic, this one with a "healer" of great potential, essentially a noble figure, who destroys himself. In Mrs. Milford's *Zelda* we find Fitzgerald and his wife destroying themselves in their complicated relationship.

The book ends with my lecture on Henry James at the University of California, Los Angeles, in 1970. Parts of it will be included in one of the two books about James which I hope to write. Here, a few passages from the lecture have been deleted, chiefly opinions about James's "major phase" by various authors who were quoted at the beginning to amuse the audience. Other slight changes have been made to reduce the lecture-platform tone and give it the aspect of an essay.

Many sentences throughout this book have been altered in the hope of improvement. A few judgments here and there have been modified, but no more than slightly. In some cases when editors have cut down the essays to fit space limitations, the excised material has been restored. Also, too many copy editors tend to invert the word order in one's clauses and give them a "came the dawn" or "backward rolled the sentences until reeled the reader" style which is unlike today's spoken language; where I've discovered such kibitzing I've changed the sentences around again.

It was fun writing all these pieces across more than thirty-six years, and I am grateful to the various editors and publishers who have so generously permitted so many of them to be reprinted in this book.

HARRY T. MOORE

Southern Illinois University
June 14, 1970

Age of the Modern

1

Psalm of Los Angeles

Now comes
The quick shy chemistry
Of California twilight.
Another moment of brightness
Before gloom hoods the sky.
In the park the restless people
Trace along the paths.
Another moment
And the trees and lake have gone dark,
And the lamp globes come alight
In a sudden multiplication of low moons
Under the cedars, under the palms.
The streets bristle with traffic from downtown
Passing the square-jawed stop-and-go sentinels
Which wink their fearful railroad colors.
And far overhead,
Other lights are coming out too,
Stars kindling in the firmament.
Who was afraid in the afternoon,
Who is a-tremble now in the night?
Now has the city become a cave of fear,
Sectored into separate infernos:
Who dares now to walk through doom
Thinking of Sargonburg at night,
Winged bulls breasting the fearful doorways,

Adelphi, March 1934.

Or Thebes in the darkness
With the stink of the river in its dead months
Coming up to the lotus-bud pillars of Karnak?
And is Wilshire Boulevard another Via Appia,
With umbrella pines and shops,
And the fields running flat to the low mountains?
Surely Wilshire belongs to those worlds,
Surely it cannot be the heritage
Of the descendants of those Spear-Danes
Whose bone-rings have been long
Powdered in the grime of forgotten middens.
Oh, did Balboa and Drake
Fail to see in the mirror of the Pacific
The hot-dog stands and oil stations of Los Angeles,
The overpaid "stars" of Hollywood,
Or the cheap-paste houses spoiling a land
That would be beautiful if left naked?
The madness goes on:
The streets are horrible in the moon,
Under the high, lion-maned palm trees,
Trees like fateful symbols of some Egyptian past—
Yet this is a large American city
With motor cars and night clubs and cinemas.
Soon these scatter the fear
And bring in its place the safe advertising-world
Of pink-faced people in gleaming clothes
Who have white-flashing, perfect teeth,
Who are expert piano players,
Who have been, one and all, superlatively educated
By correspondence courses.
And here only Jeffers cries out against it,
Mourning
My own coast's obscene future,
While all the canneries
And studios and real-estate companies
Do their best to make it more obscene,
While armies of Iowans are lured westward
To the magazine-cover paradise.
And what do the exploited Mexicans think

As the trains bump them back to their own country,
Their bodies only spools of bruised nerves
As they return to their first peonage
With none of the gold of El Dorado in their pockets?
And do our own poor fare any better,
Standing empty-eyed along the sour gutters?
Let us leave the city,
Thebes, and the tempting in't, before we further
Sully our gloss of youth.
Later, when even the listerine-lifebuoy-pepsodent people
Have tired, and have folded themselves
To rest between immaculate, crisp pages,
Fear comes up again.
The moon is out full,
Shining on Wilshire,
Shining between the silent eucalyptus trees
That stand guard by the tar-pits of La Brea,
Where tigers and mastodons once roved.
And the moon is shining on the far mountains,
That are like the young finger-shaped mountains of Italy:
The moon is beautiful if met in the upthrusting hills,
But here in the city it is a leprous thing,
Its glow blanching the rows
Of low, earthquake-fearful houses
Till they stand like white tombs
And at last
The city looks like a necropolis in the hollow night.

2

Anatomy of Chicago

Meyer Levin's *The Old Bunch* is a long, full-packed story of some two dozen Jewish boys and girls from Chicago's West Side who break away from the orthodoxy of their fathers (tailors, pawnbrokers, small manufacturers) and follow the currents of American life during the Jazz Age, the Coolidge prosperity, and the Depression. It is a collective novel, centered in the group rather than in any individual, and it presents a compelling account of the spiritual and financial plunder of Chicago.

The characters in the book are almost all decent human beings at the start, but the system they come up against is so overwhelmingly rotten that it spoils all but the very finest of them. Most of the boys become lawyers or doctors, but one important character is a sculptor and another a six-day-bicycle racer. Their lives become mixed up with many elements: parading school teachers, Al Capone, Samuel Insull, union organizers beaten by police Red squads, evicted tenants in the poor districts, Big Bill Thompson, official doctors trying to stifle news of the dysentary epidemic during the Century of Progress Exposition and, loud and swelling, the obscene chorus of the law courts with their tricky lawyers and political-machine judges. One of the most fascinating sections of the book concerns a group of doctors who form their own medical alliance despite disbarment

The Old Bunch. By Meyer Levin. The Viking Press. (*New Republic*, April 7, 1937. Reprinted by permission.)

and attacks by the official medical confederation, which is as acidly censured here as the "McGurk Institute" is in Sinclair Lewis's *Arrowsmith*. Some of the book's most important symbols are chemico-medical, and the dysentery blooms out of them most effectively.

The Old Bunch is written in hard-driving colloquial prose and is full of sharp characterizations, though the cinematic shuttling of episodes makes it hard for the reader to find characters of the kind that usually appear in fiction. The book suffers from defects of the kind which hamper most collective novels, chiefly in a lack of psychological depth. John Dos Passos attempts to make up for this in his own books and achieve a subjective balance with his "Camera Eye" interludes; here, Meyer Levin provides subjectivity in the delineation of his sculptor, who even goes to Palestine in quest of himself. The topical references which establish time are in some instances skillfully handled, but over the stretch of nine-hundred odd pages, their use often seems too much of a trick.

But on the whole this is a very readable novel, with the speed and lustiness and brawling of what is at present the world's fourth-largest city. The final direction of the author's intent comes in the form of a vision to the finest man in the book—humorless, capable, single-minded Sam Eisen, who has refused to become a shyster like his compromising friends and is something of a pariah from their respectable world, a radical. On the last night of the Century of Progress Exposition, Sam sees the bright cardboard fair as the symbol of what Franklin D. Roosevelt has given to the people. But the fair cannot last forever, and there is prophecy in the way the drunken mob is frenziedly tearing it to pieces.

3

Dorothy Richardson's Journey

It took Dorothy Richardson twenty-five years to complete *Pilgrimage*. She began the first volume or "chapter" in 1913, and it was published two years later as *Pointed Roofs*. This and subsequent parts of the novel, coming out at unpredictable intervals during and after the 1914–18 War, attracted a little band of readers who almost religiously followed the progress of the work, a task which of itself imposed some of the rigors and vigils of a quest. The twelfth and last section (*Dimple Hill*) is printed for the first time in this complete edition, which also has a 1938 explanatory foreword that announces the end of the journey. The appearance of this edition must have come as a surprise to those who had been watching Miss Richardson's work as closely as it was possible to do in recent years—the volumes were being issued less frequently in England, and the latest ones were not being published in America. The world was changing violently, and literary trends and interests were changing with it. There was even a story to the effect that Miss Richardson had abandoned her work before it was finished. So this bold "complete set," newly printed, glowing with jacket testimonials by other authors, has the emphasis of a resurrection.

The designated end of *Pilgrimage* may not altogether kill the rumor that Miss Richardson had decided to give up

Pilgrimage. By Dorothy Richardson. Alfred A. Knopf. 4 vols. (*New Republic*, April 13, 1939. Reprinted by permission.)

her work before she could bring it to a conclusion. But no definite finale was ever promised, and the early volumes gave no hint of what is usually called "form" and provided no basis for it. Miss Richardson seems to have intended to do only what she has done.

Her work has been noted for its revelation of essential feminine experience, which she presents as occurring in a flow that creates its own laws and its own form. (She thinks the phrase "stream of consciousness" inaccurate.) Her complete expression of the problems of femininity—femaleness would perhaps be a better term—reaches beyond technical matters; nor is it best realized in the obvious incidentals, such as chats about hats and drapes or the rendering of woman's point of view. It is found most importantly in the consciousness of the seemingly autobiographical main character, Miriam Henderson. Miriam believes that the art in which women are superior is that of creating atmospheres, and she feels that as a woman she has a special vision: "Shakespeare did not know the meaning of the words and actions of Nerissa and Portia when they were alone together, the beauty they knew and felt and saw, holy beauty everywhere." This secret feeling of the radiance of everything is what keeps Miriam going through her commonplace days as a teacher, as a governess, as a dentist's secretary—and makes her series of inconclusive love affairs endurable.

But whether Miriam's story is worth two thousand pages and a quarter of a century's writing is a question for debate. For Miriam never develops. The reader gets a cumulative list of Miriam's traits and comes to know her moods and what knowledge she picks up, so that Miriam becomes a "character," though never a very sympathetic one: she is intelligent (a feminist and a rather futile socialist) but she is also inhibited, fussy, self-absorbed, really neither normal nor heroic. And the other people in the story are only seen like the towns we pass in an express train; even though there are occasional brief stops we never get more than a hasty glimpse of their suface features. Miss Richardson evidently has a life-is-flux philosophy; perhaps it would have been more effective if presented in fewer books. *Pilgrimage* becomes tiresome to read because it takes up epic space without having epic design.

Miss Richardson's real talent, which is lyrical, enables her to evoke the spirit of pre-1914 London with exemplary skill. Now and then *Pilgrimage* has a green flash of country, and there is that dazzling excursion to Oberland which provides Miriam with a symbolic standard by which to judge the rest of life, but mostly the novel has yesterday's London in it: nearly every page seems lit by the harsh gaslight of Bloomsbury lodginghouses. *Pilgrimage* is superbly written, and can always be dipped into with pleasure, as if it were a good anthology of poems. But how much more we may say of Proust and Joyce, who at first seemed to be going in the same direction as Miss Richardson. Their work is similar to hers in several important respects: like her they are deeply responsive to atmospheres, like her they have experimented with consciousness-effects, and like her they have a sensitive autobiographical character who plays an important part in the story. But consider how much more Proust and Joyce have done by adding other characters, objectively conceived and drawn, and by establishing a background full enough for social understanding. Miss Richardson has not extended her work beyond the range of the individual.

4

The Great Unread
(D. H. Lawrence in 1940)

D. H. Lawrence died exactly ten years ago, on March 2, 1930. Since then he has been the subject of more legends (excepting perhaps his namesake who set off the Arab revolt) and of more books than any writer since Byron. In the case of D. H. Lawrence the personalia have impeded response to the man's writings. Everyone knows *about* Lawrence, yet his books have been for the most part neglected. During his lifetime the press helped to give him an unwholesome reputation, and this did not encourage libraries to buy his books. Shortly after his death there was a false-dawn of interest in his work: *Lady Chatterley's Lover* (1928) was still having its first exciting circulation, and the bizarre early memoirs told just enough to drive their readers to Lawrence's own books for more information about him. But, though in one form or another they contain practically everything to be found in the memoirs, Lawrence's writings are literature rather than gossip: those looking for extraneous material were disappointed when they got lost among the magnificent passages. Then the plethora of later memoirs, the trivial anecdotes and passion-prompted judgments of all the rival camp followers, made the whole subject a bore. Lawrence has remained The Great Unread.

Lawrence started out to be a somewhat traditional novelist. With his almost Dickensian knack of turning out

"The Great Unread." (*Saturday Review of Literature*, March 2, 1940. Copyright by The Saturday Review Company, Inc.; renewed 1967 Saturday Review, Inc. Reprinted by permission.)

the kind of characters formerly called "humours," and with his gift for evocation of landscape in something like the Hardy manner, he might have made himself the most successful British author of his time—if he had stuck to the path he was supposed to follow. But after the exploration of his own past in *Sons and Lovers* (1913), Lawrence felt he had gone as far as he could in the direction of poetic realism. *The Rainbow* (1915) marked the beginning of his search for a new way of consciousness, and during the rest of his life—through ill health, bitterness, and neglect—he continued that search. He came to advocate a return to man's estate before the human consciousness had felt the effects of overintellectualization. He found his ideal contemporaries among the peasants of the Mediterranean fringe, men and women who still lived under the spell of the "dark" blood-consciousness rather than in the control of the "white" mind-consciousness. In Mexico, Lawrence liked to feel "the fatal greater day of the Indians" and forget "the fussy, busy lesser day of the white people."

Certainly it would be hard to object to most of the goods he proposed for humanity—saner sex attitudes, more sunlight for more people, and so on—though a great part of the positive side of his philosophy was confused and offered no consistent program. While a man such as Lawrence must not be taken too literally, it should nevertheless be remembered that he could not even organize his friends and disciples into the Lorenzomorphic community he hoped to found. And as far as the general public went, Lawrence's soundest recommendations had the disadvantage of being poetically expressed or put forth with a prophetic gesture, so they were received with suspicion. Political developments since the time of his death have helped to create another accusation against him: there are superficial resemblances between some of Lawrence's ideas of mystic leadership and some of the Nazi doctrines, but they are only superficial resemblances. Lawrence came to see the "leader-cum-follower relationship" as a "bore" and a "cold egg," and the charge that Lawrence was philosophically a Fascist is refuted by the livingness of the whole body of his work. And in any critical estimate Lawrence's work should be considered in its entirety, with the poems, plays, and essays complementing the novels. The assembled whole will be seen to have a form which the individual units are often criticized for lacking— it has a beginning, middle, and end, and tells a compelling story of a modern man's futile struggle for integration, first in a family torn apart by social and sexual conflict, then in a world he thought was being ruined by the mechanization of human values. In its despair and frustration it is one of the great tragic stories of our time, though with its vitality and brightness it is often one of the intensest and gayest, and for sheer poetic surge of storytelling it would not be easy to find its literary equal.

If civilization ever reaches a point where the return to a precivilized consciousness is desirable, Lawrence the prophet may be resurrected, but at present Lawrence's greatest potential value is as a writer, a poet. Readers who deprive themselves of the experience of Lawrence miss some of the finest presentations of the physical aspect of the modern world that can be found in literature. Lawrence with his sense of "the spirit of place" projected into his books memorable descriptions of the mine-blasted English Midlands, of Bavarian forests, of Italy, Australia, Mexico, New Mexico. He wrote spontaneously, with little or no correction, and the sentences poured out of his pen like lava, hot and penetrating. There is nothing so demonstrative of his writing-power as direct quotation. In a few strokes Lawrence could pitch us into the heart of Mexico, as in this passage from *The Plumed Serpent* (1926) —

> Morning! Brilliant sun pouring into the patio, on the hibiscus flowers and the fluttering yellow and green rags of the banana trees. Birds swiftly coming and going, with tropical suddenness. In the dense shadow of the mango-grove, white clad Indians going like ghosts. The sense of fierce sun and almost more impressive, of dark, intense shadow.

When Lawrence introduces an old peddler into this setting, he provides us with more than just a notation of the peddler: "Silently appears an old man with one egg held up mysteriously, like some symbol"—and the picture will stay with us forever. All Lawrence's stories read like this, have this magic sense of life; his people do not inhabit a black-and-white world of print and paper, but the vivid world we see about us in life. Lawrence's vision is an intensifying one: it has its "secret," a secret he revealed once—in an essay called "The Novel" in one of his neglected books, *Reflections on the Death of a Porcupine* (1925)—and that secret was primarily Lawrence's sense of the "quickness" of life. This is a feeling for "the God-flame in things" as opposed to the dead; quickness "seems to consist in an odd sort of fluid, changing, grotesque or beautiful relatedness." A table in the room where he is writing is dead: "It doesn't even weakly exist. And there is a ridiculous little iron stove, which for some unknown reason is quick. . . . And there is a sleeping cat, very quick. And a glass lamp that, alas, is dead." Lawrence believed that "the man in the novel must be 'quick' . . . he must have a quick relatedness to all the other things in the novel," to snow and silk hats as well as to God and toothpaste.

"Quickness"—Lawrence found the correct word to describe the most elusive yet the most intrinsic element in his own writing. Within a few years the tramplings and drum-calls of new conquests may obliterate most of the traces of him as well as of many another author, but it is not difficult to imagine a day in the far future when Lawrence's "quickness" will speak for him. It will not matter whether or not the men of that new day accept him as a prophet: the livingness of his writing will speak for him, and his work will be called back, as Melville's was, among the living.

5

The Worlds of Lanny Budd

Upton Sinclair's American reputation as a novelist has been at low ebb for some time, but now in 1940 his new book should bring him back to attention in a tidal rush. *World's End* is in scope and setting partly reminiscent of two novels which were widely read a few years ago, Robert Briffault's *Europa* and George Santayana's *The Last Puritan.* Once again we have an enormous background for what must be called the education of a modern young man. The last third of the novel deals with the 1918–19 Peace Conference, a subject novelists have for the most part let alone. (John Dos Passos' *1919* touches the Conference only periphally.)

Lanny Budd, the central character in *World's End*, is thirteen when we first meet him, and only nineteen when we take final leave of him. His youthfulness as the protagonist of such a book as this is offset in great measure by his old-child wisdom: brought up among adults, he has spent his early life on the French Riviera, with his mother, who tells him when he is fourteen that she is not a divorcée after all, and that he is illegitimate; but Lanny is already sophisticated beyond the point of being shocked. Yet in another

World's End. By Upton Sinclair. The Viking Press. (*Saturday Review of Literature,* June 15, 1940. Copyright 1940 by The Saturday Review Company, Inc.; renewed 1967 Saturday Review, Inc.) And: *Between Two Worlds*. By Upton Sinclair. (*Saturday Review of Literature,* March 22, 1941. Copyright 1941 by The Saturday Review Company, Inc.; renewed 1968 Saturday Review, Inc. Reprinted by permission.)

way he is receptively young, a fresh-visioned and effective center for the story. The two young friends he has at the first, an English and a German boy, both slightly older than he, fight for their respective countries in the World War. Lanny remains neutral, for he has been given an insight into the Machiavellian origins of the war by his father, an armament maker who visits the boy frequently and even employs him at times.

Lanny keeps in touch with his warring friends, who early in the book are interestingly seen in their native settings. Though only glimpsed in the later parts of the story, they remain believable characters. Lanny's prewar visits to a "Christman-card castle" in Silesia and to an English country estate are excellent travelogues which the intermittent play of the sociological searchlight improves rather than spoils. Lanny's wanderings take him as far as Greece and over to New England, where he stays with his father's family during the time America is in the war. The picture is consistently a full one: if we have revealing close-ups of Sir Basil Zaharoff, we also encounter some of the downtrodden; if we briefly see some elder statesmen, we meet Isadora Duncan and hear Lincoln Steffens's table talk. The Peace Conference itself is a fascinating subject, and Lanny has an inside view of it, even a certain amount of influence.

No one could at this point reasonably disagree with the author's attitude toward the Conference and the Treaty, which in the main represents the average man's as well as the historians' verdict, though if this book is intended to be ammunition for pro-isolationist argument in the America of 1940, there will probably be many readers at this moment of history who will quarrel with that.

When Upton Sinclair is content to be just a storyteller he can be a compelling one, though the novelist's requisites of style, psychology, and sense of form have never been so completely developed in him as they might have been if his urge to be a pamphleteering romancer had not interfered. The limitations of mere story-gift plus idea become apparent toward the close of this book, when some of Sinclair's enduring faults trip him up and cause the novel to end with insufficient force. Lanny's experience with the police touches the edge of danger, but the reader cannot help feeling that there will be a deus ex machina for the Budd heir: the final situation lacks the power to be the climax which the mind expects from a book of such scope. And the savage argument in the closing pages is unfortunately carried on by the two characters in the book who tend to seem the least real, Lanny's father and uncle. Ironically, both men see the same causes for the war, but the munitions maker and the socialist draw widely different conclusions. As characters they sometimes too obviously symbolize philosophies battling for the allegiance of modern youth. But most of the book represents Upton Sinclair at his energetic best as a storyteller. The episodes of adventure and romance, together with the whole sweeping world-picture, provide our difficult days with reading that absorbs the mind and provokes thought.

Between Two Worlds, Upton Sinclair's sequel to his *World's End*, deals again with the experiences of Lanny Budd, the illegitimate son of an American munitions maker. This time the action swings between the 1919 Peace Conference and the 1929 stock-market crash. Lanny, after leaving the Conference in disgust and returning to his mother's villa on the Riviera, finds it hard to remain detached from world affairs, for the involvement of his friends and the partiality that events themselves seem to have toward Lanny keep him continually entangled. Once he is even expelled from Italy for political reasons.

The story throughout presents the dilemma of the man of good will in our time. Art plays a significant rôle in Lanny's case, for both music and painting are important in the lives of those about him and blend into the life of leisure and laissez-faire to which Lanny's mother and his high-caste mistress try to hold him, succeeding except for Lanny's intermittent outbursts into "pink" utterance and activity. Lanny's situation is greatly complicated, shortly before the end of the book, by his marriage to the most fabulous of

American heiresses. She is an excellent girl, and the two of them beat down the early difficulties of her marriage to a man of merely moderate wealth, as Lanny now is. The reader by this time knows Lanny well enough to be aware of the "worm i' the bud" and to wonder what Mr. Sinclair's next installment (and the 1930s) will do to this marriage.

The preceding volume had the advantage of being built around the Peace Conference which dominated the last third of the book. Here the action is more scattered. And although it is difficult not to appreciate Upton Sinclair's views of recent history, it is impossible for one to refrain from observing that his hero has to be the most incredibly opportune of all tourists to be in Rome the day Matteotti is kidnapped, in Munich during the Beer Hall Putsch, and in New York at the time of the stock market catastrophe. And to make Lanny's experience of the epoch complete, he must have no less a person than Isadora Duncan throw herself at him with the cry, "You have thrilled me to my deepest recesses!"

This is more inept, however, than most of the episodes in this all-too-episodic novel. Some of them, such as Lanny's painfully exciting elopement with the heiress, display the author at the top of his storytelling skill. But Upton Sinclair has a lesson to learn which should also be learned by Robert Briffault and Compton Mackenzie, who have been writing novel-sequences amazingly similar to this one in structure and scope. The lesson is that in these tremendous fictional attempts to convey so much of the life of a period, the single hero who remains as consistent story-center cannot successfully unify so much mass. This was known by Balzac, Tolstoy, and Proust, the greatest novelists who have used the large-size social canvas.

6

Poetry on Records

A poet reading his own work is an important event because "the sound of poetry is part of its meaning," as Gordon Bottomley said in rephrasing an old truth. By vocalizing the material, the poet can provide the listener with a unique interior comment on it. That statement is not mystic but scientific, for although the poet may not remember the original impulse and intent of every phrase (v. the case of God and Robert Browning), they are nevertheless contained in his unconscious. This is true whether the poet is an unskilled reader or a capable reciter. His tempo and his crescendi, his vocal italics and his caesurae, are all important registers toward essence.

This of course suggests problems for other vocal interpreters than the poet himself: how closely should the poet's pace and accentuation be followed? Part of the answer may be found in the area of music, where composers who conduct and record performances of their own works are rarely copied precisely by other conductors. Certainly a poet who records his own verse is not trying to shackle other possible interpreters, though in reading his own work aloud, the poet is presenting evidence that cannot altogether be disregarded.

The Library of Congress album (Number 3) of T. S. Eliot's readings includes *The Waste Land, Ash Wednesday,*

"Poetry on Records." *Poetry*, September 1949 and March 1952. Copyright by Harry T. Moore, 1970.

and some shorter poems. Eliot recites *The Waste Land* in the controlled chant fashionable today, and with the nerve-weary voice which the "feel" of the printed verse suggests. He introduces variety into the reading by occasionally dramatizing and characterizing. He even falls into cockney when necessary, though without the consistent realism of a West End actor, who would surely not forget to drop all the *h* sounds instead of merely some of them. But the listener would hardly want a stagey perfection from Eliot in such matters; much of the appeal of his reading comes from the little flaws, for they show that in spite of the general suavity of his presentation, he is essentially a platform amateur. Consequently the total effect of the reading is enhanced, for Eliot becomes at one level a man trying to tell us about his poetry, and the occasional hitches suggest sincere blunders rather than a trained artificiality; they seem to take us nearer intuitionally to the heart of the poet.

Eliot begins *The Waste Land* slowly, almost school-masterishly, a little uncertain-seeming despite his years of reading this material aloud in public (I first heard him at U.C.L.A. in 1933). But gradually the reading increases in pace and intensity, and the net is drawn around the listener. Assume that this is a trained listener, one who has been through the commentaries and has some kind of interpretational approach: these records will particularly ensnare him. And perhaps its is not only the initiates whom Eliot's reading will move: the effect may be somewhat similar upon those who, following the provided text as the records turn, are making their first acquaintance with *The Waste Land*.

The reading of *Ash Wednesday* is effective in quite another way—a measured narrative affirmation without melodrama or unctuousness—and those who are not in sympathy with the religious writings of Eliot should recall the statement, in his essay on Dante, that one doesn't have to agree with a poet's beliefs in order to enjoy his poetry.

Eliot also records, in this set, "Sweeney among the Nightingales" and two little "landscapes," as he calls them, "Virginia" and "New Hampshire." I wish there were space to discuss these in detail, to point out unexpected emphases and tones which surprise the listener and occasionally suggest interpretations which the printed versions of the poems cannot always supply.

Professor Frederick C. Packard of Harvard was the first to record Eliot reading his own work, and in these pages before I went into service in the war I reviewed his *Harvard Vocarium* disc containing "Gerontion" and "The Hollow Men" (*Poetry*, October 1940). Now Professor Packard has produced four other Eliot records.

One of these items will, like *The Waste Land*, create a special expectation among the Eliotians: "The Love Song of J. Alfred Prufrock." I was a little surprised to find Eliot reading this "straight," having expected that he might have touched it up into more of a characterization and that he might be deliberately hesitant in his utterance, almost to the point of a beginning stammer. This was not an unreasonable expectation since, as explained earlier, Eliot does "act" when he feels it necessary. But in "Prufrock" he apparently wanted to take his tone from a deeper basis than the imitative-naturalistic. And, perhaps Eliot's everyday voice is after all the correct Prufrock voice.

We find an extreme contrast to all this in the "Fragment of an Agon" section of *Sweeney Agonistes*, for Eliot reads the short lines with a comic verve, accentuating their tin-pannishness. He uses the technique of music-hall songs to suggest the surface life of modern cities, the newspaper consciousness, the Sweeney group's escape-dream into noble savagery, all recited here with a fox-trot energy that drives home the essential horrors.

The quiet reading of "A Song for Simeon" and "The Journey of the Magi" on another of the Harvard discs further demonstrates Eliot's versatility as both poet and reciter. "The Journey," after its impressive Lancelot-Andrewes beginning, goes on to become one of Eliot's vividly imaged poems and, like the "Simeon" piece, sounds all the more effective because of the carefully understated presentation. A still further contrast occurs in the record containing "Difficulties of a Statesman" and "Triumphal March." In these, Eliot dramatizes again, and his excited inflections carry in them the disorder of our politics, the problem of leadership, and the confusion of the people. The sociological force of these two poems, together with Prufrock's truncated projections of love, the religious exaltation of *Ash Wednesday*, and the concentration of modern dilemmas in *The Waste Land* reveal Eliot as one of the widest-ranging and deepest poets of the modern world: add to this the essential poetic gift, the ability to flesh the thought in music. All of this is brought out emphatically on these records.

Columbia has turned out one of the most remarkable of all poetry recordings: Edith Sitwell's plangent recitation of her *Façade* poems to the accompaniment of William Walton's music, famous in its own right and obtainable separately on records. Miss Sitwell's readings, extremely popular during her American tours, are a sophisticated attempt to restore the bardic incantations (*Façade* had first been performed in Aeolian Hall in London in 1923). Her skill in the manipulation of sounds is not limited to composition: she may have her tongue in her cheek during a good part of her rapturous performance, but if she has, it doesn't interfere with her performance.

Another poet skilled at reading his own verse, e. e. cummings, appears on two records. One, issued by Linguaphone, contains the Mr. Vinal poem, the lines on Buffalo Bill, and several other of this poet's comic pieces, all of which he reads neatly in a voice whose very inflections seem to have archly raised eyebrows. There is another recording by cummings in the Library of Congress series, *Twentieth Century Poetry in English*, which presents his recitations of "plato told" and "my father moved through dooms of love."

These poems are in Album 4 of the series, an album which also includes Robert Penn Warren, William Carlos Williams, and Theodore Spencer, the last of whom reads five poems which might be called metaphysical ballads, using themes and symbols of childhood to convey adult meanings. Most of the poems are in short-breathed measure, one of them going for nearly fifty lines in rarely used dimeter. Spencer's reading, precisely right for this material, was one of careful ease.

A quite different type of reader in this same set of records, Robert Penn Warren recites two of his poems, "The Terror" and "Pursuit," in the accent of his native Kentucky. This introduces a welcome note of variety, for the audible readings so valuable to the health of poetry should not be limited to the "Eastern," semi-English pronunciation of the Spencers and the cummingses. Yet, in matters beyond accent itself, Warren is too unskilled a reader to be completely satisfactory, for his phrases tend to clog and he has no sense of *enjambement:* he often stops as for a traffic light at the end of a line although the sentence runs on into the next line. This criticism of course applies in no way to the poems themselves, two of Warren's finest, or to the poet's compositional ear, but only to the recitation.

Reading of this kind, somewhat unskilled, sometimes has (as in Robert Penn Warren's case) a grainy honesty that recommends it to the poet's admirers, who in many instances prefer it to a seasoned smoothness. There is also a third type of presentation, exemplified in this Album 4 by William Carlos Williams. Like a number of his fellow poets, Dr. Williams has, through frequent experience of reading aloud, achieved an almost professional facility; yet his recitation does have amateurish stretches, when he lapses into monotony and the slurring of syllables. Dr. Williams loses a good deal when reduced to voice alone. I attended one of his performances at Harvard, and I watched and heard him record this disc in Washington (Robert Penn Warren kindly invited me to do so when he was Poetry consultant at the Library of Congress). I find that I miss the visual humor that goes with Dr. Williams's readings, the mischievous grins, the gestures of hand and of eye. His record is nevertheless an important one, and it is truly representative of the poet's work, for it ranges over nearly a quarter-century of his development, from "Peace on Earth" (1913) to "The Yachts" (1935), providing an interesting survey of his career before the *Paterson* phase.

The remaining poet in the album, Robinson Jeffers, will disappoint many who admire his lines in print, for he has a meager voice that scratches its way past tightened throat-muscles and gives the listener kinaesthetic agonies along his own vocal cords. Jeffers reads "Oh, Lovely Rock," "The Beaks of Eagles," and "Ossian's Grave," and they make for painful listening. But if Jeffers cannot help his own cause vocally, he has a valuable paraclete in Judith Anderson, who in a Decca recording gives a notable performance in Jeffers's version of the *Medea*. Supported by a capable cast, Miss Anderson is an effective Medea, as she was on the stage, and like many teachers I have found this "free rendering" of Euripides a valuable accessory in teaching Greek drama.

D. H. Lawrence made no recordings of his own poems, but his widow Frieda Lawrence has read five of them for an album issued by J. S. Candelario of Taos, New Mexico. The legendary Frieda, with her exuberance and her enthusiasm for her husband's work, reads "Autumn at Taos," "Red Wolf," "Invocation to the Moon," "Bavarian Gentians," and "The Ship of Death." Unfortunately, although the last two of these poems are among Lawrence's finest, the album in general doesn't give more than a suggestion of his range; it might have included "Snake" and perhaps one of his youthful *Love Poems* or *Amores* and one or two of the later, satiric *Pansies*. But we have what we have, and it must be said that Mrs. Lawrence's German accent is not a handicap in her reading. She is not a trained reader, but when she occasionally makes a slip it doesn't jar her: she goes unselfconsciously on, chanting the poems with what can only be called ecstasy.

7

An Ernest Hemingwaiad

Sing, Goddess, if you must, but be polite:
We mourn for Slugger Hemingway tonight.
The Oak Park Mauler had a big first round,
But now he stretches gasping on the ground.
Clean visioned when he started his career,
He punched out prose demotic, terse, and clear,
Each sentence plain American and rough,
The speech of those who at least pretend they're tough.
For literary ancestors take Twain
And Ringgold Lardner, with their brisk disdain
Of parlor language, genteel and sedate,
Which their coarse idiom helped exterminate:
Twain's Huckleberry Finn and Lardner's stories
Were body blows to stun linguistic tories.

When young, the hopeful, striving Hemingway
Learned journalese the Kansas City way;
And the fading slugger, Sherwood Anderson,
Taught Hem some tricks and then was turned upon:
He showed the mauler how to dodge and swing,
And for reward was dunked in torrents of spring.
The aspiring champ next trained with Gertrude Stein,
Who kept the hypertense young pug in line;
And Ezra Pound helped curb the mauler's antics
With sharp advice on the footwork of semantics.

Encounter, June 1958. Reprinted by permission.

And when Hem wrote of problems in our time,
He started on his tantalizing climb
Up that forbidding, high, and lonely wall
From the top of which the Humpty Dumpties fall:
For he who quickly mounts too soon forgets
That the same sun which rises also sets.

      Yes, in the twenties Hem was the coming champ,
And imitators thronged into his camp.
They copied Ernest's every little trick,
Though he alone could make the style click.
He spawned a school that at its roaring best,
As Eastman said, wore false hair on its chest.
And yet, for all its loud ineptitude,
The school had caught one thing, a widespread mood:
A host of exiles, disillusioned cubs,
Left midwest cornfields for exotic pubs.
And quickly Hem, war vet and refugee,
Composed their Iliad and Odyssey.
His book imported to our blushing shores
The Left-Bank carousel of drunks and whores,
And modern Fisher Kings with blood-tipped spears,
Castrati fighting back their absinthe tears.
Bullfighters, too, whose tight-green sexual pants
Drove high-placed, bobbed-haired ladies to romance;
And men sans women, keen to fish again
In the big two-hearted river of Michigan.
Hem even wrote the first good gangster tale
Before the films made thugs the dream-boat male.
And when war books were not yet in the fashion,
Hem made them so with his neat tales of passion;
The reading public fell before the charms
Of lovers making their farewell to arms.
This novel hit again the modern note,
The woman speaking through a tightened throat:
"You've had no other girls? You're lying now,
But keep on lying, darling"—this is how
The love-scorched nurse talks to her paramour:
"Oh darling, you've a lovely temperature!"

But this compelling novel, like good wine,
Requires no bush, no advertising sign,
For in this century of super-wars,
It makes most other battle-novels bores.

But in writing it, Hem almost shot his wad,
For afterward his habit was to nod:
And now for his lost talent there's bereavement.
A few short stories pieced out his achievement,
A few good tales that lurked yet in his pen;
But his novels seemed by nature's journeymen.
Two tales of Africa he'd still to tell,
Of Kilimanjaro's high and snow-topped hell,
And Macomber, who lost his shaking life
When he redeemed himself before his wife.
And a few shorter stories kept the pace,
The best set in a clean, well-lighted place.
Hem's bullfight book of death by afternoon,
The author's first nonfiction honeymoon,
Became a minor classic of its kind,
Though the old lady left the bulls behind
When she inquired in blank astonishment
Just what those words with the four letters meant.
The green-hills book of Africa was no success,
For most reviewers made a bloody mess
Of trying in dense jungles to pursue
The magic and elusive gold kudu.
And then the novels, the remaining four:
How paltry after what had gone before!
The once-great slugger, trim and disciplined,
Was getting punch-drunk, heavy, short of wind.
A lively *Cosmo* piece that had a plot.
Concerning Cuba, smuggling, and a yacht
Was stretched beyond its strength to tell the story
Of hard-boiled Harry Morgan's spurious glory:
This earnest man, this Bogart-Garfield of
The fishing boat, fake cargo, and hot love.
By now, one fact was emerging like a crescent:
This author's main ideas stayed adolescent.

And then the next book with its tolling bell
Rang out a fading talent's further knell.
The earlier Ernest would have told this tale
In a hundred pages, neat and on the nail.
The people here go in the cave, and then
Go out and in, go in and out again,
With all the weary regularity
Of their reciting of the word *obscenity*.
Occasionally the author hits his stride,
The death of Sordo on the mountainside,
And the murder of the fascists in the town,
Though so much sadism weighs the story down.
And as for ideology, or where
The hero stands, the book does not declare:
For him the Spanish war becomes a jag
Of cuddling "Rabbit" in the sleeping bag.
And though at last Roberto blows the bridge,
A grim fate stymies him upon the ridge.
But at least from all the phony prose he's free:
"I obscenity in your obscenity"!

The second war found Hem upon the scene
To write hack stuff for *Collier's* magazine;
We all now hoped the talent wasn't blunted.
But then, instead of the masterpiece we wanted,
We got a colonel with a cracking heart
Who tore the winning generals all apart,
Then crossed the river to the farther trees,
Where there was no more fondling of the knees
Of his extremely young and hot contessa.
She had become both Stella and Vanessa
To ageing Colonel Cantwell, whose banal
Complaints would overflow the Grand Canal.
He called her Daughter as he stroked her breast
And relished this display of fake incest:
A way to be emotionally thrifty,
Unharnessing such notions when you're fifty;
Though for this colonel, love so barmecide
Turned out to be a form of suicide.

And Hemingway himself was sprawled supine
While all the critics counted up to nine,
But just before his seconds tried removal,
He bounced back up again to win approval.
His brave old Cuban with his tattered fish
Was at last the critics' and the readers' dish,
Though some declared this fable was the thing
Another writer once called "Jesusing":
Hem went from heroism dramatized
To heroism sentimentalized,
And old admirers once more had to pine
For the Hemingway of 1929.
Today if you've a story, drool it, sir,
And that'll help you toward the Pulitzer.
As for a grander, more exalted height,
Where Lewis and O'Neill are on sight,
Remember it was climbed once by the truck
Of Mrs. Pearl Sydenstricker Buck.
And there was also William Faulkner's rise
From Popeye's corncob to that Nobel Prize;
Americans get up there, with their hustle,
At younger ages than a Shaw or Russell.
But as his old admirers surely know,
Our Hemingway seemed punched out long ago,
Though now and then he throws a line to rope us
In to expect that promised magnum opus,
The time when finally our ageing boy
Lives up to his boasts and tangles with Tolstóy.
Alas, each day that day seems farther off,
And now when we think of Hemingway we doff
Our hats, and though he might regard us dopes,
We grieve for shrivelled prose and blasted hopes.
So, sing, Goddess, if you must, but be polite:
We mourn for Slugger Hemingway tonight. . . .

8

D. H. Lawrence
Love as a Serious and Sacred Theme

At last a publisher in one of the English-speaking countries has dared to bring out the full text of our century's most astonishing romance, which has for too long been a smugglers' trophy. It is D. H. Lawrence's *Lady Chatterley's Lover*, written in the twenties.

In the novels of contemporary writers of a stature comparable to Lawrence's, love is usually treated shabbily, as something perverse, ironic, or merely annoying. But his book dealing with love as a serious, major, and sacred theme has been taboo here and in his native England for the thirty-one years of its existence. Meanwhile, a mutilated edition that sells chiefly as a drugstore paperback has parodied what he really wrote; this emasculated version omits Lawrence's faithful descriptions of the love experience and his use of the four-letter words in the special way which he believed was therapeutic. His own attempt to neutralize *Lady Chatterley's Lover*, at the suggestion of his publishers, had ended in a cry of "Impossible! I might as well try to clip my own nose into shape with scissors. The book bleeds."

After he began selling it by subscription, from Italy in 1928, the novel was pirated in America. Since then, the authorized editions printed in English on the Continent have supplied American tourists with a spicy bit of contra-

Lady Chatterley's Lover. By D. H. Lawrence. The Grove Press. (*New York Times Book Review*, May 3, 1959. © 1959 by The New York Times Company. Reprinted by permission.)

band to sneak past the customs. The underground reputation of this book, whose essential innocence should long ago have been quietly accepted, has given it an unfortunate emphasis—unfortunate because, unlike James Joyce's *Ulysses*, whose own forbidden-fruit days gave it a lurid excitement for a time, *Lady Chatterley's Lover* is not its author's masterpiece. Earlier Lawrence novels such as *The Rainbow* and *Women in Love*, produced at the summit of his writing power, stand out as far better books. Yet, though they have romantic ingredients, *Lady Chatterley's Lover* occupies a special place in the Lawrence canon because it is exclusively a romance.

We may now see clearly that it is the authentic descendant of *Madame Bovary* and *Anna Karenina*. But instead of leading his heroine to her doom, Lawrence shows her the way toward renewed and enriched life. Here, as in so much of his other work, he creates his own variant of the Sleeping Beauty myth, in which a woman in a trancelike state of unfulfillment is awakened by what might be called the Erotic Invader. In story after story ("The Fox," "The Ladybird" and *The Virgin and the Gipsy* are typical), the Erotic Invader breaks through the thorny hedge of an imprisoning relationship to release the dreaming woman or "lost girl."

Lady Chatterley, like so many of Lawrence's stories, is set mostly in the English Midlands. Once again, as the symbol of his antagonism to industrial civilization, he used the mines which blight the earth there and, in Lawrence's view, blighted human beings also. But in attacking industrial civilization and its mechanization of the living, which often took the form of the intellectualizing of natural impulses, Lawrence was not trying to destroy what he called "mind knowledge" but to bring it into balance with "blood knowledge" of the kind celebrated in *Lady Chatterley's Lover*. He made his position clear in his notable essays, *A Propos of "Lady Chatterley's Lover"* and *Pornography and Obscenity*, as well as in letters such as the one quoted in Mark Schorer's illuminating introduction to the present volume: "You mustn't think I advocate perpetual sex. Far from it. . . . But I want, with *Lady C*, to make an *adjustment in consciousness* to the basic physical realities."

In a different letter, Lawrence explained that as a young writer he had heard an older author (Edward Garnett) say he would "welcome a description of the whole act," and that this had stayed in his mind until he wrote *Lady Chatterley*. Some critics have attacked this naturalistic impulse in the book because it tries to express what they think is the inexpressible. But after numerous readings others find (as I do) that Lawrence's endowments as an artist—his incandescent gifts as a prose writer, his command of cadences and verbal impressionism—did him more than yeoman service in expressing the very difficult.

He didn't limit himself to naturalism in *Lady Chatterley*, which has the therapeutic overtones mentioned earlier. At times, too, the writing has the quality of sacrament, though that is less apparent here than in many of Lawrence's other works. He once thought of calling this novel "Tenderness"—and tenderness is the key to the story.

Only a reading of the book can reveal its power, its depth of complication, its psychological and social intricacy, all of which contribute to the effectiveness of the long slow process which the gamekeeper and the lady of the manor go through in order to find enrichment in love. Without so full a development of the people and the situation, the love descriptions would be meaningless. So would the unleashing of the four-letter words by Mellors, the gamekeeper, in the presence of Constance Chatterley—words intended to root out and purify feelings long hidden by shame.

The flaw of the novel doesn't lie in this direction but rather in the physical crippling of Sir Clifford Chatterley, who comes home from the First World War smashed and impotent. This is a weakness in the story not because it sets up an apparatus for sentimentalism over the betrayal and desertion of Clifford, but rather because it has the effect of removing the target which Lawrence was most of all aiming at. This was the overintellectualization of such people as Clifford, a colliery owner who becomes a clever writer of the "mind-knowledge" type. Lawrence would have strengthened his story if he had shown that it was such elements, which can exist in men not physically crippled, that drove Connie into the arms of his gamekeeper, the preserver of natural life. Even if this is not Lawrence's finest book, this over-the-counter edition of the full story may have the virtue of encouraging more people to read Lawrence's other novels, his essays and his poems. *Lady Chatterley's Lover* justifies itself, if not necessarily as a healing book for all readers, at least as our time's most significant romance.

9

Kay Boyle's Fiction

In her latest novel about Americans abroad, Kay Boyle writes of their interaction among themselves and Germans in 1948, the third year of the occupation. It is a story that once again demonstrates this author's skill at managing dramatic tensions in a context of symbolism.

From the time of her first book in 1929, *Wedding Day and Other Stories*, her fate has been occasional high praise and an occasional succès d'estime. Meanwhile, writers far less gifted have been overrated by public and critics alike. At present there are only a few books of Kay Boyle's in print; these fortunately include a hardbound edition of her novel *Monday Night* and paperbacks of *Thirty Stories* and *Three Short Novels* (the last containing one of the masterpieces of this genre in our time, *The Crazy Hunter*). Of her first novel, *Plagued by the Nightingale*, it is safe to say that it is the finest portrait of a French family by a writer from this side of the Atlantic since Henry James fixed his attention upon the Bellegardes in *The American*. Nor is it out of place to mention James here, for Kay Boyle is an important later practitioner in the area in which he worked—"the international theme." Since James, no American except Kay Boyle has concentrated so thoroughly upon that theme.

Despite the excellence of the results, however, Kay Boyle's writing career has had some severe setbacks, partly

Generation Without Farewell. By Kay Boyle. Alfred A. Knopf. (Kenyon Review, Spring 1960. Reprinted by permission of Kenyon College.)

attributable to timing. She learned to write in the 1920s, when craftsmanship was important, but by the time she began turning out her full-length novels the Depression was on; instead of her subtle penetration of the behavior of Americans in Europe, readers over here wanted what seemed to be the only realities of the moment—rough stories of hunger marchers, factory slaves, or dispossessed tenant farmers. It was a time when entire social classes, rather than individuals, were of dominant interest in fiction, and it was a period when the autobiographical novel was not fashionable; consequently it didn't help Kay Boyle's cause for her to have, in most of her books, a sensitive American girl as the reflector of the action, which usually involved a group of expatriates. Now it may be seen (and I hope it will be seen) that these novels were not indulgently self-centered, not mere personal chronicles, but were rather the reworking of significant experience into fable, intensified by a prose style at once delicate and forcible. Some of these novels were well received, for there have always been intelligent readers who can look beyond the fashions of the moment, but there was no big sale and no spreading critical excitement. And now (except for *Monday Night*) Kay Boyle's fine novels of the 1930s are all out of print: besides *Plagued by the Nightingale*, these include *Year Before Last, Death of a Man, My Next Bride*, and *Gentlemen, I Address You Privately*. They deserve reprinting [and, since this review was written, *Plagued by the Nightingale* and *Year Before Last* have been reprinted in the Crosscurrents/Modern Fiction series].

Unfortunately, after her return from Europe during the Second World War, Kay Boyle began bending her high talent to the production of the fictional fudge of *Saturday Evening Post* serials, with results that were unsatisfactory from the point of view of her early admirers—and probably the readers of popular magazines were not very much pleased either, since a certain amount of subtlety remained amid the melodramatic scenes. In 1944, at a time when Edmund Wilson was exerting great influence with his *New Yorker* causeries, he came upon one of Kay Boyle's serials,

Avalanche, published as a book, and he brought a weight of ridicule down on it. Reprinted in his brilliant volume *Classic and Commercials*, this essay has continued to damage Kay Boyle's reputation across the years. But it should have risen again with *The Smoking Mountain*, her first book about Germany, which came out in 1951. This collection of stories and sketches was certainly the finest volume of fiction written by an American, up to that time, about Europe after the war. And now, *Generation Without Farewell*, which expands several of the themes of the earlier book, is a worthy successor. Its quality is certainly far beyond the range of other novels about postwar Germany, such as Donald Davidson's *The Steeper Cliff* (1947), William Gardner Smith's *Blood of the Conquerors* (1948), or Clay Putnam's *The Ruined City* (1959)—all of them competent novels, posing moral problems in dramatic situations (Smith's book adds the Negro dilemma), but none of them more than just competent. *Generation Without Farewell* exists in a realm beyond them.

Its Germany is haunted alike by its Gothic and Nazi past and its American present. Most of the Americans in the story, whether well meaning or not, are essentially childlike. They include an army colonel who brings in his wife and college-girl daughter; a post-exchange manager whose Italian ancestry seems to offend the colonel; a sycophantic lieutenant; a marmotlike intelligence officer; and an *Amerika Haus* director named Honerkamp, whose nonconformist thinking is "dangerous"—a man who has hanging behind his office door the *Totentanz* figure of a skeleton found buried in the ruins.

The central consciousness in the story is that of a young German newspaperman, Jaeger, who has been a prisoner of war in the United States. And several of the other characters are Germans, including a young groom who watches over the white Lippizaner horses which (as in Kay Boyle's notable short story, "The White Horses of Vienna") suggest the aristocratic splendor of the past. There is also the battered young actor who presents the Wolfgang Borchert play from whose words this novel takes its title: "We are the generation without farewell . . . We have many en-

counters, encounters without duration and without farewell."
This applies to most of the relationships in the book, particularly to that of Jaeger and the colonel's wife. He falls in
love with her and she responds, but she is abruptly sent away
with her daughter, who in her quiet way has also been drawn
into Germanic involvements. The colonel hustles his women
off before they have a chance for farewells.

This Colonel Roberts, who is suggestively identified with
the boar that is rumored to be raiding villages at night,
shares a triumph with the intelligence officer when, at the
end of the story, the *Amerika Haus* liberal is given dismissal
orders. All such events have their parallels in the dark
conflicts that take place in the forest where the colonel
leads patrol parties by night to track down (ostensibly at
least) the illegal hunters reported to be prowling the area
in a jeep with covered-over license plates. There are violence and bloodshed in this forest but, since this is among
other things a symbolist novel, the meaning of it all is not
spelled out so facilely as in a popular type of book such as
The Ugly American. Many of the same meanings that book
drives toward are ultimately to be found here, however, particularly American incompetence in dealing with other nations. Colonel Roberts in this story is the embodiment of
the military mind, essentially uneducated and incapable of
growth, that has so often damaged America by mixing in
government, for which it is untrained and temperamentally
unsuited.

These points come to mind because this book is—for all
its symbolic bestiary of boar, fox, and Lippizaner horse—also
a political story, with politics and symbolism blending in an
unusually successful way. For example, the terrible symbol
of the buried man, which has a certain kinship with Honerkamp's office skeleton, is political. This "underground" man,
accidentally dislodged from the ruined house where he has
been immured for three years (a place stocked with food),
is seen by Jaeger as he emerges.

It moved like a spider caught in its own web, like a broken
crab, clawing its way up through rusted girders and disjointed
stones. . . . The rags of a *Wehrmacht* uniform clung to the

figure's bones, the sleeves, the trousers hanging in shreds, slashed back and forth and up and down by outraged time.

Several men had been similarly unearthed in different parts of Germany, but to see one is a new experience for Jaeger who, in writing about the event for his paper, says that every German now "must claw his way out of the depths of what he was, letting the faded, filth-encrusted insignia fall from him, and the medals for military valor drop away." But a defeated chauvinism has been taken over by new chauvinists, and the military mind of the conquerors has no tolerance for the Jaegers or the Honerkamps, who at the last are either frustrated or defeated.

This book is not one of narrow-visioned propaganda; rather it is a later and richer chapter in Kay Boyle's continuing involvement with the international theme, which in our time has new phases. And perhaps this novel will bring her some of the recognition she deserves and will help to place her among the fine women authors of our time who do not write like men (as, say, Willa Cather does), but operate through a distinctly feminine vision (as Dorothy Richardson does), to capture and project experience in a unique and important way.

10

The Return of John Dos Passos

A writer seldom retrieves a long-lost reputation at a single stroke, but John Dos Passos has probably done just that with *Midcentury*, by far his best novel since he completed the *U.S.A.* trilogy with *The Big Money* in 1936. It is written with a control of narrative styles, a grasp of character, and a sense of the American scene. In its fictional passages this panoramic novel recaptures the Dos Passos verve and intensity of a quarter-century ago, while the background sections, made up of sociological tidbits and pertinent biographical sketches, show much of the old Dos Passos skill at manipulating the devices which helped to give *U.S.A.* originality and force.

The fictional heart of *Midcentury* contains several simultaneously developing stories. At first the emphasis falls upon three men closely involved in union activities. The garrulous Blackie Bowman, onetime Wobbly and former resident of Greenwich Village, is now confined to a bed in a veterans' hospital, where his reminiscenses—vintage Dos Passos—go backward through the century. Terry Bryant, who fails to reform his union, takes to taxi-driving as a last refuge of individualism. Frank Worthington collides with union troubles similar to Terry's, but surmounts them to become an official far enough removed from rank-and-file

Midcentury. By John Dos Passos. Houghton Mifflin Company. (*New York Times Book Review*, February 26, 1961. © 1961 by The New York Times Company. Reprinted by permission.)

reality to fail to see the merits of Terry's case when it briefly crosses his attention.

In repeated, vigorous, and one-sided attacks on labor unions, Dos Passos hammers away at racketeering of the kind we all know exists. But he hardly suggests that there are good as well as evil unions. About three-fifths of the way through the volume, however, when the antiunion poundings threaten to become tiresome, he introduces two new and interesting characters, Jasper Milliron and his son-in-law, Willoughby Jenks, who take part in exciting battles at management levels where the villainy of unions is only incidental. In adding this dimension, Dos Passos proves again that he can write about business—which doesn't have to be a dull subject—better than anyone since Theodore Dreiser. The sequences concerned with it in *Midcentury* are worth a dozen grey-flannel-suit and executive-suite novels. Here the author gives fictional life to some of the phases of American civilization recently noted by popularizing sociologists, but he does so with pronounced individuality and the stamp of authority. If the sociologists look, with a scientific eye, at outwardly directed and herd-motivated men, Dos passos regards them with deep pessimism and gloom—here projected fictionally in the downfall of Jasper Milliron and in the ensnaring of Will Jenks in an unhappy compromise.

Not that Dos Passos has ever been a cheerful writer. He began his career in the early 1920s with two despairing war books, long before such novels became fashionable. In 1925 his *Manhattan Transfer* displayed a gallery of unhappy city dwellers, but readers hardly noticed the mood of the book as they admired its cinematically shuttling episodes. This technique was elaborated in the "collective" novels comprising *U.S.A.*, which perhaps didn't really champion the masses so much as this author's enthusiasts of the time thought they did, but rather celebrated individualism.

With his next trilogy, *District of Columbia*, completed in 1949, Dos Passos suffered a loss in critical reputation and, presumably, in readers. It wasn't merely a matter of disagreement with the opinions he set forth, but rather, in most cases, with the excessively dogmatic and story-spoiling way in which he expressed them. *District of Columbia* and the novels following it lacked the concentrated power of *U.S.A.* and gave their readers almost no hint that the author had left in him the kind of imaginative energy that manifests itself in *Midcentury*.

In this volume the interstitial *U.S.A.*-style biographies reappear, beginning with one of Douglas MacArthur that is mostly favorable though acidly critical of the general's intelligence service at Clark Field and on the Yalu. Another military man, General William F. Dean, is portrayed as a hero for his resistance to brainwashing while a war prisoner in Korea. Mrs. Roosevelt receives only a few ironic jabs; the picture of J. Robert Oppenheimer is largely sympathetic. What begins as a portrait of Freud becomes too much a cartoon of headshrinkers, while Sam Goldwyn when shorn of his Goldwynisms seems almost "included out." The sketches of two senators involved in labor investigations, John McClellan and Robert M. LaFollette, Jr., point up the differences between their personalities and methods. Most of the biographies focus on labor leaders such as John L. Lewis, Harry Bridges, Walter Reuther, Dan Tobin, Dave Beck, and James Hoffa, and under the circumstances a few of them seem to escape rather lightly.

In place of the inward-searching camera eye of *U.S.A.*, *Midcentury* offers seven intermittent investigator's notes, antiunion testimony delivered to a shadowy figure, and although these may reflect a good deal of truth they become rather tedious. On the other hand, the interludes which are here called documentaries recapture a good deal of the liveliness of the earlier trilogy's "newsreels" in their blaring headlines and spasmodic reflections of background events. These documentaries feature references to space travel, armament, schizoid patients, and other appropriate topics which, like the biographies, give perspective to the imaginative sections.

The prose of *Midcentury* has fewer color shadings than the earlier volumes. But it is recognizably Dos Passos' in its sparing use of the commas that hook a reader's eye and in its Joycean ramming together of words ("a shortnecked grayhaired man"). The writer's distinctive cadences are also noticeably present, in the choral chants of the biographies and, more emphatically, in the hard-surfaced narrative passages and in the crackling realism of the dialogue, all of it good American-built writing.

The ministerial side of Dos Passos, which never lets him tell a story for its own sake, also appears here. In the fictional sections concerned with Jasper Milliron and Will Jenks, however, the novel doesn't drum its lessons home so obviously as in the antiunion sermons, but lets the dramatization do its own work.

Jasper's entrance into the story is preceded by the biography of the railroad magnate, Robert R. Young who, like Jasper, couldn't cope with the forces working against him. Jasper wasn't born early enough to have established a strong position in the rough-enterprise era, and in his fifties he is squeezed out of his high executive position with a milling company by men who represent the newer phase, scimitar instead of bludgeon.

Will Jenks, trying to operate a taxi company in defiance of a monopoly, has for an associate the Terry Bryant who earlier in the book became a taxi driver as a form of self-expression. Even though Terry is murdered in the cab war, Will wins it; but his victory is Pyrrhic. He can consolidate his position and go forward only by merging with his defeated rivals, subsidiary of a car manufacturer, whose monopoly he had tried to break.

In these stories Dos Passos is apparently trying to show Americans what is happening to their vaunted individualism in this age of conformity and conciliation. The man of originality, the voice of singleness, the spirit of independence—he seems to be saying—will be defeated at every level of our national activity; you no longer can fight 'em, you have to join 'em.

As if this isn't a frightening enough prospect, he ends the book with a disturbing suggestion of the future in the person of Jasper's adolescent nephew-by-marriage, a Holden Caulfield type named Stan Goodspeed, whose story is balanced by the biography of the teen-agers' fetish, the late actor James Dean. Stan, who among other things typifies American rootlessness, is last seen on a cross-country spree, which he finances by stealing credit cards belonging to Jasper, whose days are now blurred by his heavy drinking.

Ironically, this book of wormwood and gall appears at an hour when liberalism seems to be again somewhat in the ascendant and when, despite warnings of stiff times and tight sacrifices ahead, most Americans are fairly optimistic. *Midcentury*, which by scrutinizing so many current problems and presenting them with the force of an effectively told story, provides material for some severe reflection. As a story, it has enough power to lift it above the imperatives of the moment and into consideration as serious literature, certainly as one of the few genuinely good American novels of recent years.

11

Henry Miller
From Under the Counter to Front Shelf

Since the day *Tropic of Cancer* first appeared in Paris as a paperback in 1934, it has been smuggled into English-speaking countries which turn their customs inspectors into censors. The high praise of such writers as T. S. Eliot, George Orwell, Edmund Wilson, and Sir Herbert Read made it contraband of uncommon quality. Now the book has at last become available in the author's native country.

It was Henry Miller's first published volume, and it is as good as anything he has turned out since. It glows with the joy of discovery: I can write! Its engaging first-person narrative, the monologue of a man who draws people to him, tells the story of an American expatriate—not a Henry James gentleman in a Place Vendôme hotel, but rather a Left Bank vagabond merrily sponging on his friends. Like him, they are members of the international semi-literary, Parisian-tenement set, and they enjoy having him around.

All of them, particularly the narrator, have frequent, erotic adventures with every type of woman from the local *poules* to rich American widows. Every bit of this is set down graphically, with precise physical details and Old English locutions employed both descriptively and conversationally. Yet, with cinematic abruptness, the narrative often switches from amatory scenes to lyric evocations of the

Tropic of Cancer. By Henry Miller. The Grove Press. (*New York Times Book Review*, June 18, 1961. © 1961 by The New York Times Company. Reprinted by permission.)

faubourg soft in the dusk or the river streaked with lights. The style throughout is plain, though always energetic and vivid, with split-angled Braquelike images rising from the hard texture of American speech.

The Miller man, here and in later books, is in effect the descendant of Dostoevsky's Underground Man, without his nastiness, and of Rilke's Malte Laurids Brigge, without his fastidiousness. Miller's hero even has his feminine ideal, the American girl here called Mona, who recurs in his other books under a slightly different name; and although he marries her, she remains elusive. Yet his hectic devotion to her doesn't stop him from having all those other jubilantly recorded love affairs.

How different Miller's books are from those of Jean-Jacques Rousseau, who designated his biography as *Confessions*—the Rousseau of paranoid snufflings, who was guilt-haunted all his life because in early youth he had let a servant girl take the blame for a ribbon he had stolen. This is not meant to detract from Rousseau's stature as a writer, but merely to point out that Miller's joyful self-exposure is of quite another kind, unhampered by guilt. The *Tropic of Cancer* man is capable of acridness, but for the most part he moves from one escapade to another with the easy, conscienceless zest of a child. It might be said of him, as Yeats said of Miller's American forerunners and true masters, Whitman and Emerson, that he lacks the vision of evil in his assertion of self-reliance, in his song of himself.

He has been a generally liberating influence upon other writers, for many of his values, particularly his reverence for life and his attacks upon standardization, have been widely circulated and adopted, if only unconsciously. Overtly, his influence is most apparent upon celebrants of rootlessness such as the beatniks, or upon Lawrence Durrell, whose later works are the outgrowth of his early novel, *The Black Book*, which in its turn is an outgrowth of Miller. Durrell says of Miller: "American literature today begins and ends with the meaning of what he has done." Of course to some readers *Tropic of Cancer*, strong language and all, may seem dated, but perhaps to many others the publication of the book here and now will reemphasize its enduring freshness.

Henry Miller, who is now in his seventieth year, was a latecomer to literature. Sometime between apprenticeship as a tailor in the 14th Ward of Brooklyn and his floating existence in the 14th arrondissement of Paris, Miller held down an executive position in the philistine-bourgeois-square world, for he put in several years as a Western Union employment manager in New York—which gives his escape into the ragged geometry of Montparnasse a special Gauquinesque flavor.

After *Tropic of Cancer* he wrote other volumes calculated to make the customs men increase their vigilance, notably *Black Spring* (1936) and *Tropic of Capricorn* (1939), which in theme and treatment are on a level with *Tropic of Cancer*. At the time of World War II Miller returned to the United States, where he brought out several "harmless" books, including *The Colossus of Maroussi* (1941), a lively account of his travels through Greece with Lawrence Durrell, and *The Air-Conditioned Nightmare* (1945), a vivid report of his wartime journeys through America. He settled in California, with little money; but suddenly the overseas G.I.'s discovered his books published in Europe, which began to sell faster than they could be reprinted.

Foreign publication continued with the trilogy *The Rosy Crucifixion* which, like most of Miller's prewar books, cannot yet be imported into the United States. *The Rosy Crucifixion*, which deals with the author's earlier New York life, tends to be monotonous in a way that the preceding autobiographies were not. In the *Tropic* and *Black Spring* volumes, the erotic sections are elaborately explicit, but they are also frequently ceremonial; the more recent books, although they contain some magnetic narrative passages and scenes of high Miller comedy, too often become a wearying chronicle of sexual acrobatics.

The question comes up in relation to all these Miller volumes and particularly *Tropic of Cancer*, the first one to be put before the general public in America: Are they—besides being anarchic, antimilitary, antiprison, antimoney and antirespectability—are they obscene? Miller himself, in his essay, "Obscenity and the Law of Reflection," quotes D. H. Lawrence to the effect that obscenity is almost impossible to define. In recent legal decisions concerning Lawrence's *Lady Chatterley's Lover*, the literary quality of the book has usually motivated a favorable verdict. Of course Lawrence had a special purpose in *Lady Chatterley*, which he intended to be therapeutic for an age he regarded as sexually sick, and it must be said that he might well have been horrified by parts of Miller's work; there are indeed tenuous distinctions along the borders of the salacious. Yet, to consider for a moment one of the great classics of vulgarity, was Chaucer ever better, in his treatment of character and situation, than in his Fescennine masterpiece, "The Miller's Tale"?

Chaucer was simply telling a story, as Henry Miller is simply reflecting modern life. And if, in the Miller essay mentioned above, he quotes Romans 14:14, in his own behalf, he is not doing so irreverently, for he is a deeply religious man and a respecter of all religions. The section he cites from St. Paul's letter to the Romans includes the famous statement, "There is nothing unclean of itself: but to him that esteemeth any thing to be unclean, to him it is unclean."

Now it must be granted that parts of *Tropic of Cancer* will hammer away at some of the strongest of stomachs, even in this epoch in which so many books are really scabrous. But in the present volume, among other things, Miller projects with gusto some of the great comic scenes of modern literature. There are, for example, the Dijon sequence in which the narrator goes to teach for a while in a broken-down provincial lycée; the last episode of the book, which involves the Miller man and one of his friends and a French family in a crazy farce; and, above all, the scenes describing a Gandhi disciple looking for fun in a Paris brothel. If literary quality is a criterion, these passages run far ahead of any considerations of obscenity; in themselves they guarantee that Henry Miller is an authentic, a significant author whose ripest work has been too long forbidden in his homeland.

12

The Language of Fiction

"Who cares for fine style? Tell your yarn and let your style go to the devil. We don't want literature, we want life." Except for the somewhat outmoded word *yarn*, those sentences might have been written by one of today's younger American or English novelists, so many of whom seem inclined to let style go to the devil. But that statement was made by Frank Norris in 1899. Norris, who died in 1902, is today honored as a pioneer of American naturalism, but his reputation cannot match that of his almost exact contemporary, Stephen Crane, who didn't have Norris's contempt for the resources of language.

As the prose of Crane and others who have mastered the medium demonstrates, effective use of style doesn't mean ornamentation, but rather an intensifying of all the organic elements in a novel or story. Intensification of this kind occurs at the end of chapter 4 of James Joyce's *A Portrait of the Artist as a Young Man*, when in a moment of high emotional significance young Stephen Dedalus sees the wading girl. Stephen, who in a recent spiritual crisis has considered becoming a priest, now realizes that his mission will be to serve beauty of another kind from that found in the Church. He admires the bare legs and fair hair of this girl to whom he doesn't speak, and in the "profane joy" of his silent, ecstatic appreciation, he becomes the artist.

"Speaking of Books." *New York Times Book Review*, September 16, 1962. © 1962 by The New York Times Company. Reprinted by permission.

It is impossible to summarize this episode adequately, for its language is an intrinsic part of its forcefulness, of its very meaning. Its visual effects, including the Dublin twilight tints, are striking, as are its sounds, particularly the evocation of the stirred waters in the repetitious "hither and thither" as the girl keeps moving her foot back and forth. This presages the river sequence of *Finnegans Wake* with its "rivering waters of, hitherandthithering waters of Night!"

Joyce of course represents only one type of prose mastery. The more spontaneous D. H. Lawrence achieves effects of a quite different kind, and many readers prefer him. Both Virginia Woolf and William Faulkner are first-rate writers of fiction who have notably dissimilar styles. And the crisp sentences of the early Hemingway have left their mark.

There is also F. Scott Fitzgerald, who was sometimes the victim of a glossy facility; but in his best writing he could, by means of an almost murderous discipline, turn this very characteristic to good use. In *The Great Gatsby*, for example, the parties on the "blue lawn" amid the "yellow cocktail music" have exactly the right color-tone for their section of the story. And at the beginning of *Tender is the Night*, when Fitzgerald speaks of the "bright tan prayer rug of a beach," this too is exactly right, for that Riviera coast is the place of ritual for the Americans in the book whose playing is their praying. At the end of the story, when their chief priest and "organizer of private gaiety," Dick Diver, is banished from the sacramental beach, he sways a little as he blesses it by making the sign of the papal cross. Fitzgerald presents this in precisely the appropriate manner, symbolically, psychologically—and stylistically.

Today, the few younger authors who attempt to write well usually succeed only in turning out a slippery novelese. But most of the newer novelists pay small attention to language and merely bang away at it with little awareness of the power of phrasing or the suggestibility of sound and color. They write a grocery-list prose.

One of these novelists who has a good deal to say but doesn't always know how to say it, in one of his books describes his hero as being "broken up." This comes at a moment of climax in the story, and that dead phrase is all the reader is left with at the end of a chapter.

One sad aspect of the present situation is that so much of this kind of writing is accepted so uncritically. Most current reviewers seem insensible to the craftsmanship of prose as they concentrate exclusively on what stories try to say—as if that element, any more than style, were detachable. Such critics seldom show that they realize that what paint is to the artist and what musical sound is to the composer, language is, or should be, to the imaginative writer. Granted, language is necessarily the vehicle of ideas, so that literary criticism must be at least partly conceptual; but language is also sensuous, in this aspect representing important qualities of the life which the storyteller is trying to express. When novelists and critics achieve a full understanding of this, our imaginative literature may greatly improve.

13

Silas Lapham
His Fall and Rise

William Dean Howells spent his childhood and youth in the then semifrontier state of Ohio, he was American consul at Venice for four years, he wrote extensively, he edited the *Atlantic Monthly*, he became the intimate of Boston's social and intellectual leaders, and then in 1888 he moved to New York for the last thirty-two years of his life. In this final period, when he was recognized as "the dean of American letters," Howells surprised his old friends and the reading public when he became at least verbally a Socialist after many years of supporting the Republican ticket. All in all, it was a life that intensely gives substance to Howells's numerous volumes, of which thirty-five are novels. Among them the most famous and most highly regarded is *The Rise of Silas Lapham*.

Published in book form in 1885, it was the first novel of scope and artistic merit to be devoted to a study of an American businessman. (The spectacular speculator of *The Gilded Age*, by Mark Twain and Charles Dudley Warner, appearing about a dozen years before *Silas Lapham*, is hardly a "businessman."). Because Howells was essentially on Lapham's side, his book contrasts, in tone and implication, with most stories of such figures in later American writing: Theodore Dreiser's wizard-financier Frank Cowperwood, say, or Sinclair Lewis's less titanic George F. Babbitt. Dreiser gave

"Afterword" to Signet Classics edition of *The Rise of Silas Lapham*. By William Dean Howells. (New American Library Editions, 1963. Reprinted by permission.)

detailed accounts of Cowperwood's villainies, though the raw forcefulness of the character magnetized his author, whose attitude toward Cowperwood became somewhat blurred. In *Babbitt*, Lewis started out to show his protagonist as a clown, but kept making him more and more sympathetic, indeed somewhat spoiling his book by this shift of attitude.

Howells had an easier time with Lapham. First of all, he didn't portray him as a capitalist monster of the Cowperwood type, corrupting public officials and gobbling up traction companies. Cowperwood cares little for human consequences, while Lapham has a tortured conscience because of his shabby treatment of his former business partner, Milton Rogers. In trying to make amends for this, Lapham brings catastrophe upon himself. As for the tribal mannerisms Lewis made fun of, Lapham shares only a few of them with Babbitt: his almost ritualistic worship of business, for example, and his indulgence in what his future son-in-law speaks of, mildly enough, as the ungrammatical. Howells, who essentially admired his Yankee businessman, kept jesting at his expense to a minimum. He reminded himself in his notebook, "Make Lapham vulgar but not sordid." Indeed, when Howells's protagonist speaks foolishly after drinking too much wine at an upper-caste Boston dinner party, he attracts the reader's embarrassed sympathy.

Howells, himself a poor country boy who had risen to fame and wealth, could understand such a man as Lapham, who had made his fortune on his family's farm in Vermont by developing mineral paint; Howells first amplified his own talent in his native Ohio. Both men owed much to their fathers: in the story, the elder Lapham discovered the mineral paint, but he hadn't his son's knack of finding a market for it; in life, the elder Howells had set his son an example by being a minor writer as well as a printer, but he lacked his son's ability to make connections with the publishers who might help him expand his talent. There are other parallels between William Dean Howells and Silas Lapham; but if the author could to some degree enter into the consciousness of his character, he could also look upon him from the outside with the eye of a realist in fiction who had become something of a proper Back Bayan.

The creator of Silas Lapham was born at Martins Ferry on March 1, 1837, the thirty-fourth anniversary of the statehood of Ohio, which had earlier been part of the Northwest Territory. In Howells's boyhood there was still a frontier, and for one year he and his family even lived in a log cabin. But Ohio was already becoming rural, and the flatland was speckled with communities of the kind that, a generation later, Sherwood Anderson knew and subsequently described in *Winesburg, Ohio*.

That helpful father of Howells was a Welshman, a Quaker who, like the father of Howells's friend-to-be, Henry James, became a Swedenborgian. The literacy of the household was augmented by the future author's mother, Mary Dean Howells, who was of Irish-German descent. She, too, was sympathetic to culture when she had time to think of it while bearing and bringing up eight children, one of whom (a boy) was insane.

Young William Dean Howells became a printer's devil, and in his teens he set up his own verses. As the family moved from town to town, the boy taught himself foreign languages. Much of his youthful poetry shows the influence of Heine, whom he greatly admired; one of the other authors Howells read in the original at this time was Cervantes, whose *Don Quixote* became the object of a lifelong enthusiasm.

In 1860, when Howells was a newspaper reporter in Columbus, Ohio, a gay, witty, and charming girl came there for a visit from Vermont, the future state of Silas Lapham. At the home of relatives, Elinor Mead expressed surprise at seeing a copy of the *Atlantic Monthly*; to her further astonishment, she soon met one of its contributors, a young newspaperman named Howells, whose poetry James Russell Lowell had published in that journal. Two years later the *Atlantic* contributor and the girl from Vermont were married in Paris.

Howells had meanwhile written one of the campaign biographies of Lincoln. He appreciated Lincoln's log-cabin background, but he didn't have the historical intuition to consider the candidate from Illinois worth a trip to Springfield for an interview. Howells engaged a friend there to collect material for him, from which he wrote a fairly good hack biography. The meager proceeds from it enabled him to make a trip to the city in which, so long afterward, Silas Lapham was to "rise." In Boston, and also at Concord, Howells met some of the great figures of what Lewis Mumford has called America's Golden Day: Hawthorne, sending Howells to see Emerson, wrote on the back of his card, "I find this young man worthy."

The Lincoln administration also found him worthy, to the extent of appointing him consul at Venice. His sojourn there roughly paralleled Lincoln's term of office, 1861–65: William Dean Howells rode out the Civil War in a gondola. This is not said in disparagement, for Howells felt guilty the rest of his life because he had missed the war. He made Silas Lapham a veteran, the colonel of a regiment. Yet Lapham's creator would hardly have been a good soldier; as Edwin H. Cady says in the fullest biography yet devoted to him, "For Will Howells, of course, military service was psychologically out of the question." He was the victim of a psychic stress astonishing in a man who was to become so healthily successful, with so finely developed a sense of the genial and the comic. But the condition existed; he was not cut out for bivouac and battlefield.

The years in Italy, largely spent sitting under the oleanders in his garden on the Grand Canal, were valuable to him, and he often revisited that country. As James L. Woodress shows in *Howells in Italy*, the familiarity that he acquired there with the plays of the eighteenth-century Venetian dramatist Goldoni taught him how to treat commonplace themes truthfully.

When Howells returned from Venice with his wife in 1865, he was determined not to live in Ohio again. After a brief spell of editorial work in New York, he went to Boston as assistant to James T. Fields, who had succeeded Lowell on the *Atlantic*. In 1871 Howells in turn replaced Fields. In his new position he encouraged and helped develop new writers, notably Mark Twain, who, like Henry James, became one of his closest friends.

Howells's first novel, *Their Wedding Journey*, came out in 1872. Before this he had written several other books, including *Venetian Life* (1866). *The Rise of Silas Lapham*, serialized in the *Century Magazine* before it appeared as a book in 1885, was his tenth novel. Among his subsequent works of fiction, *A Hazard of New Fortunes* (1890) ranks highest.

That story, reflecting Howells's move back to New York two years earlier, also reveals its author's growing interest in social-reform movements. This was not evident in *The Rise of Silas Lapham*, for although this book deals rather intricately with business, the problems of labor do not play the important rôle they so emphatically assume in *A Hazard of New Fortunes*, published only five years later.

At the beginning of *Silas Lapham*, Howells indulged his habit of introducing characters from earlier novels. As the story starts, the newspaper reporter, Bartley Hubbard, familiar to readers of Howells's finest previous novel, *A Modern Instance* (1882), is preparing to interview Lapham for the "Solid Men of Boston" series. Hubbard died in the earlier book, so the reader familiar with Howells's work knows at once that *Silas Lapham* goes back somewhat in time; the exact date of its beginning is 1875, when Lapham is fifty-five. Hubbard, whose irresponsibility and caddishness are indicated by a few deft strokes, is in this later novel only a minor functionary, merely a device for the introduction of the central character. In the interview, Lapham tells of his impoverished farm background, at once exaggerated by Hubbard, of his father's inability to capitalize on the mineral paint he discovered on the land, of his own brief adventures in the Southwest and, finally, of his marriage to a Vermont schoolteacher and his founding of the paint company that has made him wealthy. He speaks also of his two daughters, Penelope and Irene. By the time the interview ends, the reader knows a good deal about Lapham. Even his appearance is projected through a quotation given in advance from Hubbard's article, which describes Lapham as a man with "a square, bold chin, only partially concealed by the reddish-gray beard, growing to the edges of his firmly closing lips. His nose is short and straight; his forehead good, but broad rather than high; his eyes blue, and with a light in them that is kindly or sharp according to his mood."

This feature-by-feature type of description is an example of the literary realism of Howells. He never went to the extremes of naturalism, either in its graphic extensions of realism or in its pessimistic determinism. "Our novelists," he said in *Criticism and Fiction* (1891), "concern themselves with the more smiling aspects of life, which are the more American." But at the same time he admitted that the condition was "changing for the worse"; indeed, "he has already written *A Hazard of New Fortunes* to prove it," as George N. Bennett points out in commenting on the quoted phrase. Nor were Howells's "smiling aspects" reflected in the work of the rising school of American naturalists. Frank Norris said that the realism of Howells, the admirer of Tolstoy and even of Zola, was that "of the broken tea cup." And certainly, despite various pictures of despair in *Silas Lapham*, including that of the desperate and broken-down Rogers, the fastidious reader will find nothing in the book that might offend him. There is a rugged gulf of contrast between *The Rise of Silas Lapham* of 1885 and the first novel by one of Howells's admirers, Stephen Crane, who only eight years later brought out *Maggie: A Girl of the Streets*.

No street girls appear in the Howells volume, whose social problems occur at other levels. (It must be said for Howells that in the uproar caused by *Maggie* he took Crane's part.) Although *The Rise of Silas Lapham* is intensely concerned with the complex of post–Civil War Boston, the story not only omits labor troubles and street girls but also fails to include the immigrants, chiefly Irish, who were crowding into the city at that time. In his social picture, Howells focuses principally on Lapham, the man of farm background, and on the Coreys of Beacon Hill. The head of that old established family, Bromfield Corey, is a highly cultured loafer, and his wife habitually refers to her Salem ancestors. Their son Tom is inclined to be democratic; he calls on the

Laphams, or at least on the daughters, and establishes a connection between the families.

The geography of this novel has an important bearing on the development of its plot. The *nouveau-riche* Lapham, not a resident of Beacon Hill, has bought property in the next-most-respectable district, the South End; but when Back Bay becomes the fashion he decides to build a house out there, "on the water side of Beacon Street." Through all this, the atmosphere of Boston is wonderfully projected. Today's reader feels at the heart of the story the city of red brick and gray plaster, with salt always in the air, the clock-clock of the horses' hooves as carriages roll along, the web of inland waterways, the aristocratic rise of Beacon Hill, the crowded harbor at the end of the city, the choked little streets of the "intown" area and, farther out, the wide boulevards with their flourishing trees. Howells suggests all this rather than presenting it graphically, but these features are there; and how tellingly Howells makes use of the social symbols of this community—what we today call status symbols. One of these is Lapham's elaborate house in Back Bay, which burns down before it has been completed and shortly after its insurance policy has expired. This disaster is only one among several that descend upon Lapham toward the end of the story.

In the earlier part of the book, Lapham wishes that he could invite young Tom Corey to work for him. When Tom of his own accord comes to the paint-company office to ask for a job, Silas immediately takes him aboard the Nantasket boat to visit the family's summer cottage. All the Laphams think that Tom is interested in Irene, who soon falls in love with him, but it is Penelope whom he hopes to marry. The situation creates some nice-mannered Victorian confusions of the kind Howells could deal with so expertly.

Much of the criticism of *Silas Lapham* (as in O. W. Firkins's book of 1924) has been directed at the love-story subplot. Various observers have found it only tenuously connected with the principal theme, which concerns the business adventures of Silas Lapham. True, the self-sacrificing sisters are rather thinly sketched, but the Lapham-Corey association gives Howells a chance to set up some interesting contrasts which have a bearing on the main plot. The very presence of the Coreys is one of the elements which make Lapham overreach himself. Today, critics tend to give more symbolic weight to the interrelationships of people in a story than aesthetic legislators did in the past: nowadays, the extra plot, which isn't a necessary part of the main theme but serves to heighten it, is often thought worthy of praise.

In the social-comedy aspects of the story, Howells is at his finest in his account of the dinner party at the Coreys'. As Mrs. Corey greets her guests she addresses Lapham as General Lapham and fails to hear his modest self-demotion to colonel. Just after this she is responsible for one of those social cruelties that could be so neatly depicted by Howells, a lifelong admirer of Jane Austen.

> A little lull ensued upon the introductions, and Mrs. Corey said quietly to Mrs. Lapham, "Can I send anyone to be of use to Miss Lapham?" as if Penelope must be in the dressing room.
>
> Mrs. Lapham turned fire red, and the graceful forms in which she had intended to excuse her daughter's absence went out of her head. "She isn't upstairs," she said, at her bluntest, as country people are when embarrassed. "She didn't feel just like coming tonight. I don't know as she's feeling very well."
>
> Mrs. Corey emitted a very small "O!"—very small, very cold—which began to grow larger and hotter and to burn into Mrs. Lapham's soul before Mrs. Corey could add, "I'm very sorry. It's nothing serious, I hope?"

At the dinner table, the conversation is somewhat beyond Lapham's range, and he keeps rather quiet while taking in a good deal of Sauterne, followed by Madeira. Then he suddenly talks too much and too loud. This ruefully comic social débâcle foreshadows his financial catastrophes.

The day after the party, when Lapham sees Tom Corey at the office, he asks, "Was I drunk last night?" After Tom has mumbled some condescending words of reassurance, he thinks ill of himself and goes to Lapham's house to apologize. Penelope greets him there, and when he blurts out that it is she rather than Irene whom he loves, the uproars

which follow make Lapham's behavior at the party seem un-
important. Now the story works toward its final complications, as Lapham's monetary troubles increase and his moral
crisis takes shape.

Lapham under stress shows that he is not a typical capitalist of the time. The action of the story occurs during the
Grant administration, when the men who have been called
the robber barons were taking over so much of the country
and its resources. Lapham proves not to be of their breed,
although he shares with some of them an attitude later to
be charted by Max Weber in *The Protestant Ethic* and by
R. H. Tawney in *Religion and the Rise of Capitalism*: business as sacrament. If Tom Corey has faith in Lapham's product, it is a secular faith, for to him the paint is merely
"the best in the market"; but Lapham has told him, "It's the
best in God's universe," and he has said this "with the
solemnity of prayer," affirming the holiness of thrift and the
profit motive.

Lapham has another characteristic in common with the
robber barons: he is what the popular sociology of today
would call an inner-directed rather than an other-directed
man. Dreiser's Cowperwood was one of the last possible
examples of the inner-directed, and *The Titan* of 1914 was
a kind of *Götterdämmerung* of the old-style capitalist. By
the time Lewis's *Babbitt* appeared, in 1922, the typical
businessman was already the helpless prisoner of tribal customs. John Dos Passos, in a later study of a business official
in an age of conformity—*Midcentury* (1961)—shows how
the creative executive, Jasper Milliron, is crushed by commit-
tees. Most of today's greyflannel-suit novels reinforce this
theme. But Lapham, like Cowperwood, could for good or
evil determine his own course of action.

Howells said he had intended Lapham's "rise to be a
moral one"; he felt that the aging Boston historian, Francis
Parkman, missed the point of the rise in thinking of it as
social. But two of the men in the story who attended the
party at which Lapham talked too much didn't miss the
point: the Reverend Mr. Sewell thought that the Lapham
who had undergone financial difficulties presented "a moral

spectacle," while the artistically inclined Bromfield Corey "found a delicate, aesthetic pleasure in the heroism with which Lapham had withstood Rogers and his temptations."

Critics have sometimes referred to Rogers, that former partner whom Lapham tries to help, as a Dickens-like character, but he also resembles one of the shabby secondary figures who so often motivate villainy in Ibsen's plays, which the later Howells admired. It is Rogers who, toward the end of the novel, makes the proposition that creates the moral crisis of the story. Lapham, before he ruins himself financially by rejecting Rogers's schemes, paces his room at night. His wife, so often his conscience, remembers Jacob wrestling with the angel and refusing to let him go until the angel should bless him. And Lapham takes at least one blessing out of his struggle, the sense of having been right. He says, when Sewell asks him if he has any regrets—

"About what I done? Well, it don't always seem as if I done it. . . . Seems sometimes as if it was a hole opened for me, and I crept out of it. I don't know," he added thoughtfully, biting the corner of his stiff mustache. "I don't know as I should always say it paid; but I done it, and the thing was to do over again, right in the same way, I guess I should have to do it."

In spite of this display of Victorian moral earnestness, the novel doesn't seem antiquated, partly because its language is simple and of the kind that doesn't date: good, clear English throughout the narrative sections and, in the dialogue, slightly flavored with Vermont or Beacon Hill locutions. Above all, the book seems fresh and lively today because, as it examines an interesting corner of our heritage, it lives up to the first and most important rule for the writing of novels: it tells a good story.

14

Oblomov
A Candidate for Dante's Fourth Terrace

Oblomov, accented on its second syllable as drowsily as you wish, is a comic Russian novel about laziness; it was first published in 1859 and written by an author whose name skips upward at the end: Goncharov.

Like Sinclair Lewis's Babbitt in modern America, Goncharov's principal character provided a term broadly applied to a social class, to a way of life. In nineteenth-century Russia, Oblomovism became a synonym for the inertia of the landed gentry. The expression has lived on into the Communist régime: the old Leninist, Nikolai Bukharin, condemned to death in the 1938 purges, said at his trial that Oblomovism was one of the afflictions of the upper orders of Soviet bureaucracy.

In creating Oblomov, Goncharov did more than manufacture a serviceable word. This character stands among the great comic figures of world literature, in whose register the book ranks as a masterpiece. But Goncharov's other works, although highly regarded in his native land, have never taken hold elsewhere. Besides poems and stories, they include a travel journal, two confessionals, and a pair of novels that their author considered on a par with *Oblomov* in presenting a social triptych of Russia in transition between 1840 and 1870: *A Common Story* (1847) and *The Precipice* (1869).

"Foreword" to Signet Classics edition of *Oblomov*. By Ivan Goncharov. (New American Library Editions, 1963. Reprinted by permission.)

Ivan Aleksandrovich Goncharov was born in 1812 in the Volga town of Simbirsk (Ulyanovsk today). His father, a grain merchant and landowner, died when the boy was seven. Young Goncharov and his brother and two sisters were brought up by their vigorous and practical mother, who kept an eye on the family business and managed the nearby estate of a retired naval officer. (Incidentally, Simbirsk was later in the century the birthplace of two future but quite different heads of the Russian government, Aleksander Kerensky and the man who took the name N. Lenin.)

As a child, Goncharov had plenty of chance to observe the operations of a small but thriving industry. He knew the creaking wagons that brought the grain into town, the dry smell of the storage bins, the flat cargo boats of the Volga, the clerks who scratched down statistics. The boy also knew, in contrast to this business activity, the life of the country estates, whose families lolled around as serfs waited on them. This opposition between the enterprise of commerce and the ease of parasitism remained in Goncharov's consciousness; it recurs thematically throughout his novels.

The retired naval captain whose estate Goncharov's mother supervised took an interest in the boy and sent him to a local school for upper-class children, where he first learned to read French and English. At ten, Goncharov went to Moscow to attend a commercial institute, at which he did poor work in the business courses but showed an aptitude for foreign languages. In 1831 he became a student of philology at the University of Moscow, where he made his literary debut a year later in a magazine that published some chapters he had translated of a Eugène Sue novel.

The University of Moscow in the 1830s bubbled with intellectual activity. The future political exile Aleksander Herzen and the brilliant critic-to-be, Vissarion Belinsky, were among Goncharov's fellow students, but he did not know them. In a memoir, Goncharov provided a brief and vivid picture of another of his university contemporaries, the poet Mikhail Lermontov, whom he saw but never met. As a student, Goncharov kept to himself and read Pushkin.

After his graduation in 1834, he returned to Simbirsk. But after several dull months as secretary to the governor of the province, he removed to St. Petersburg where, as a member of the civil service, he became a translator and subsequently a censor. He suffered through an unhappy love affair in his youth and never married. He retired from his government post in 1867, with a pension, two dozen years before his death.

This sounds like an uneventful life, aside from its literary aspects, but it has quaint corners of interest because Goncharov was an odd fish. Some of his peculiarities, which increased with the passing of time, will be discussed further on.

Just now it is time to consider his first novel, *A Common Story*, which began appearing as a serial in the pages of an important journal, the *Contemporary*, early in 1847. In the preceding year Goncharov had at last met his former fellow-student, Belinsky, who now praised the story highly in the *Contemporary*, and this contributed to its success.

In that first novel Goncharov contrasts two men, an uncle and a nephew, the first of whom lives amid the lively noisiness of St. Petersburg and the second on a quiet country estate. The bucolic young Aleksander Aduyev is a dedicated romantic, full of extravagant ideals and hopeful rhetoric. When he goes to St. Petersburg, his uncle Peter, who is both a bureaucrat and a manufacturer, schools him in worldliness. One of his lessons consists in transforming the manuscripts of Aleksander's poems into wallpaper. Several years and several unhappy love affairs later, Aleksander goes back to the provinces, which, after St. Petersburg, no longer have their idyllic appeal. He returns to the capital and becomes a successful bureaucrat—balding and paunchy, and engaged to a rather commonplace heiress. His transformation seems to be a denial of romanticism—Belinsky saw this as the direction of the story—but the ending blurs into ambiguity because Goncharov shows the sophisticated uncle puzzled as to whether or not he has taken the right path, along which his nephew has followed him.

Like all of Goncharov's fiction, *A Common Story* is an

elongated sketch rather than a narrative filled with the kind of action usually found in novels. Its descriptions are Flemish in their attention to detail, an element that prompted Belinsky to compare the book with Dostoevsky's recently published *Poor Folk* as an example of the newer realism.

In 1849, two years after *A Common Story*, Goncharov published in the *Contemporary* a tale called "Oblomov's Dream," which he labeled as part of an unfinished novel. Completion of the book lay eight years in the future, publication ten. Meanwhile—in 1852—Goncharov went on a long sea-voyage as secretary to the vice-admiral commanding an expedition the Tsar sent out for the purpose of opening trade relations with Japan. Because the Suez Canal was not yet built, the travelers took the long way around to reach the Pacific, with stops in Denmark and England. In 1854 Goncharov had to go back to Russia from Japan because of European political crises, including the Crimean War. He returned by land, an adventurous journey in those days before the Trans-Siberian Railway. His letters from abroad and the diary he kept became the basis of *The Frigate "Pallas,"* first published in full in 1858. This was essentially a logbook, and most of its accounts of faraway places are perfunctory and dispirited.

Goncharov was, however, a frequent traveler. He made several visits home to Simbirsk, whose atmosphere permeates a good part of his fiction, and he often went abroad. He finished *Oblomov* at the spa of Marienbad in 1857, two years before it came out in the *National Annals*. This was a conservative journal, unlike the *Contemporary*, which had become increasingly radical. But it was the *Contemporary* that exploded with enthusiasm for the book.

Before this happened, *Oblomov* had not received much praise. Ivan Turgenev's *A Nest of Gentlefolk*, which had appeared in the pages of the *Contemporary*, had hitherto been regarded as the important novel of the year. But the critic for the *Contemporary*, twenty-three-year-old Nikolai Aleksandrovich Dobrolyubov (Belinsky had died in 1848), at once saw the possibilities of *Oblomov*. He drew particularly upon the term "Oblomovism," used in the book itself, as a weapon of ridicule against the landowning class.

Another ten years passed before Goncharov's next novel came out. Although *The Precipice* was plotted and partly written before *Oblomov* was finished, Goncharov did not have his third novel ready for print until 1869. Its central character, Boris Raisky, is a dilettante who is indecisive about which form of art to take up. In a Volga province where an estate at the edge of a cliff gives Russian literature one of its most spectacular landscapes, Raisky realizes that he loves his cousin Vera. She finds the exiled nihilist, Mark Volokhov, more attractive, but she marries the practical merchant Tushin. None of these characters has the force of Vera's grandmother, who represents the older Russian type, tightly bound to custom and tradition. But even this graphically portrayed old woman cannot prevent *The Precipice* from being Goncharov's poorest novel, diffuse and often dogmatic.

No one was on hand to praise it when it appeared, for Dobrolyubov, like Belinsky, had died young. The lukewarm critical response to the book embittered Goncharov, who thought it was his masterpiece. In several essays published posthumously we find him justifying the novel, as in one work he brought out during his lifetime: the confessional *Better Late Than Never* (1879; written 1870). He also prepared a counterpart to this confessional, *An Uncommon Story*, whose title ironically echoes that of his first novel. He left instructions that *An Uncommon Story* was to be published after his death only if lies and rumors about him appeared in the press—lies and rumors that this document would supposedly annihilate. It went unpublished until it was brought out under Soviet auspices in 1924. It screams with *la folie des grandeurs*.

And that is the secret of Goncharov's peculiarity—a manic state far more discomforting than mere Oblomovism. During Goncharov's lifetime, as in his posthumously published book, his paranoid condition manifested itself most strongly against his friend Turgenev, of whom Goncharov became violently jealous. When Turgenev's *A Nest of*

Gentlefolk made its appearance in 1859, Goncharov accused him of plagiarism. He said that in 1855 he had given Turgenev a full account of *The Precipice*, which was then in progress. In 1860, when Turgenev brought out his next novel, *On the Eve*, Goncharov once again charged him with having stolen parts of *The Precipice*. Turgenev, who in his time quarreled with Tolstoy and Dostoevsky, asked a group of fellow authors to arbitrate this case of supposed plagiarism.

The accused, the plaintiff, and the referees all met at Goncharov's quarters, in what is surely one of the weirdest conclaves in literary history. Turgenev explained firmly that he would never betray the confidences of a friend, a remark and an attitude that Goncharov, in *An Uncommon Story*, sneered at as "mummery." Later generations have agreed with the verdict of the artibrators, who found that any similarities in the works of the two writers were coincidental; both stories had rural settings and reflected the ideas of the time.

Four years later, Goncharov and Turgenev were reconciled, but only temporarily. The slow-writing Goncharov could not control his envy of the more productive Turgenev. His sense of being persecuted intensified, as a letter written to his publisher in 1868 shows: Goncharov complained that he was sick, haunted, and misunderstood, and that his closest friends insulted him. He now kept his manuscripts locked up so that Turgenev or his "spies" couldn't steal ideas from them. Goncharov felt that Turgenev not only used these himself but also passed them on to other writers, who profited from them: Berthold Auerbach in *The Country House on the Rhine* and Gustave Flaubert in *The Sentimental Education*. There is comic irony in Goncharov's suspicions of the latter book, for later critics almost invariably compare his first novel, *A Common Story*, not only to Balzac's *Lost Illusions* but also to Flaubert's *The Sentimental Education*.

Goncharov's attitude toward Turgenev was responsible for at least one appalling scene. In a park in St. Petersburg, when Goncharov saw his "enemy" in the distance, he ran in the opposite direction screaming, "A thief! A thief!"

In his last miserable years he cut himself off from almost all human associations. Only his German valet could see him; after this valet died, only his widow and her children had access to Goncharov. He was fond of them and remembered them in his will. He was partially blind in later life, and in 1888 he suffered a stroke which left him nearly helpless. He died three years later in his St. Petersburg flat. In several ways his death, like parts of his life, resembled Oblomov's.

And of course Oblomov was largely a self-portrait. In *Better Late Than Never*, Goncharov says that he took the lazy image of Oblomov from himself and his observations of others. Similarly, Aleksander Aduyev, in *A Common Story*, and Boris Raisky, in *The Precipice*, are autobiographical figures, and the books in which they appear are reflections of a somewhat limited experience and a vision concerned more with the psychological than with the social.

As to the social aspects of Goncharov's three novels, critics in and out of Russia since his time do not concur with his view that these books are essentially a social panorama of the country in transition; one point these commentators bring up is that Goncharov scrambled his characters in a way that makes some of them anachronistic in their milieu. And the interpretations of Oblomov's character made at the time by Dobrolyubov are not so readily accepted as they once were. Dobrolyubov labeled Oblomov as one of the futile heroes of Russian literature, along with Pushkin's Onegin, Lermontov's Pecorin, and Turgenev's Rudin. Later observers have pointed out that Onegin, Pecorin, and Rudin are activists beyond the farthest-ranging dreams of Oblomov.

Rejecting some of the earlier findings, later critics tend to greet Oblomov as a remarkable literary character in his own right, as part of a particular and peculiar tradition. It might be added here that torpor of different kinds, real or assumed, yawns its way through the literature of the world. Joe, the fat boy in Dickens's *The Pickwick Papers*, can go to sleep anywhere, at any time. If Jonson's Volpone stays in bed as part of a masquerade of dying, Molière's Argon imagines that he is himself an invalid (it is important to note that

Goncharov felt he had affinities with Molière). The narrator of Proust's long novel at last finds refuge between the bedcovers, as his creator did in life. In Huysmans's *Against the Grain*, Des Esseintes is so deeply wrapped in ennui that he cannot take his proposed trip to the England he admires, so he stays in Paris and dreamily projects himself through the paces of the voyage. As for Walter de la Mare's "poor tired Tim," the poet tells us that "it's sad for him," mooning and moping through the day and then creeping off to bed "too tired to yawn, too tired to sleep." Cases abound. Most of these characters who are driven bedward have some kind of psychological defect, and Ilya Ilych Oblomov hardly constitutes an exception.

He would not seem a comic figure in all times and places. In medieval western civilization, for example, sloth was a sin. In his *Divine Comedy*, Dante, punishing those who succumbed to sloth while on earth, puts them in Hell with the wrathful and the envious, condemning them to gurgle forever in the sour marsh of the fifth circle. In his *Purgatory*, Dante forces those who are purging themselves of *accidia* to keep running desperately around the fourth terrace. Today we usually regard laziness more as an inconvenience than as a crime, and we rarely take stronger action against it than ridicule—though totalitarian states discourage inertia, at least by doctrine. Bukharin's application of the term Oblomovism to the Soviet hierarchy was doubtless meant to be a powerful insult.

The psychological emphasis of *Oblomov*—the concentration on idiosyncrasies of an individual character—is far from a denial that there was certainly a good deal of lassitude among the upper classes of Goncharov's day; to a certain extent, Oblomov himself symbolizes this condition as well as the ancient Russian tendency toward resignation. We find these elements in the works of other Russian writers; they are used somewhat differently, for example, by Chekhov, whose three sisters, despite all their talk, never go to Moscow, and another of whose indolent families takes no positive action to prevent the cutting down of its beloved cherry orchard. But, once again, in the case of Goncharov's novel, the focus is more personal than social. Indeed, the social aspects of *Oblomov* are incidental or, it might be said, accidental, since Goncharov once admitted that he was not aware of them until Dobrolyubov had pointed them out. Fortunately, in writing the book, Goncharov had no tendential urge, as he had in *The Precipice;* he could feast on his hero's mannerisms and oddities.

Appropriately enough, *Oblomov* begins with its central character in bed, his natural medium, his principal vehicle on the journey between womb and grave—a journey involving, for him, as little motion as possible. Oblomov, whom we first see in his early thirties, has resigned from civil service employment because it has put pressures of responsibility on him. Living in a St. Petersburg flat, he is the absentee landlord of a country estate whose baliff takes advantage of his master's indolence and fleeces him. When Oblomov learns from his own landlord that he must vacate his quarters in the city, the idea of a household move so demoralizes him that he forbids his servant, Zakhar, even to discuss it. Such is Oblomov.

Yet he emerges as a likable character. The fumbling, dirty old Zakhar bullies him but remains affectionately faithful to this zany master. There are further testimonies to Oblomov's attractiveness in that he has numerous visitors—Mohammeds coming to the mountain. As they keep entering and leaving, they make the opening section of the book seem like the first act of a play whose author introduces a variety of people early in the game. Now it is true that these visitors are for the most part self-centered and self-seeking, yet they do come to see Oblomov, and they are friends of long standing. To evoke Dostoevsky's *Crime and Punishment* may seem farfetched, but there is similarity in the techniques each of these authors uses to create sympathy for his protagonist. Dostoevsky's Raskolnikov, after committing his murders, lies feverishly in bed and treats with surliness the friends who come to see him; nevertheless, they continue to like him, even after the facts about the murders become known—the idea emerges that Raskolnikov is, in spite of his ferocious deed, essentially what we would call a nice guy. *Oblomov*, appearing seven years earlier than *Crime and Punishment*, has at least this point in common with Dostoevsky's book: its bed-bound hero attracts a horde of visitors.

And, for all his sluggishness, the genuinely harmless Oblomov has strong humanitarian feelings. He tells one of the early callers, the author Pyenkin, not to forget in his writings that thieves and prostitutes are human beings and should not be cast out of society. This anticipates the generosity of feeling Whitman manifested in his address "To a Common Prostitute," in which he says,

> Not till the sun excludes you do I exclude you,
> Not till the waters refuse to glisten for you and the leaves
>   to rustle for you, do my words refuse to glisten and
>   rustle for you. . . .

It may seem extravagant to find anything in common between Goncharov's lethargic Russian and the deliberately hearty Whitman (who knew, however, when to loaf and invite his soul), but the humanitarian sentiments are shared, and may be noted as part of Oblomov's character.

In the ninth chapter of Part One of the novel, Goncharov inserted the piece originally printed in the *Contemporary* as a separate unit: "Oblomov's Dream." This soft lyric glides Oblomov back into his protected childhood, amid gentle sunlight and pleasant irresponsibility. A pre-Freudian dream, this detailed and wishful reminiscence is another key to Oblomov's character.

Zakhar ends the particularly joyful bit of slumber by dutifully and firmly waking up his master at half-past four, at which moment a figure out of Oblomov's childhood comes in: Andrei Stolz. This practical half-German friend finds Oblomov's slothfulness shocking. It is he who coins the term Oblomovism, and he bustles the fatigued man out of bed in order to drag him around to parties. When Stolz leaves for western Europe, he makes his friend promise to meet him in Paris, which he of course doesn't. But Oblomov undergoes a new and transforming experience: Stolz has introduced him to the lively Olga Ilyinsky, and Oblomov falls in love with her.

How he now behaves and what is the outcome of this new emotion are matters that Goncharov deals with in whimsical detail, as in the case of another relationship of Oblomov's — the one with Agafya Matveyevna. The story suggests a question: Is it possible for a man of inaction to find a woman who is sufficiently impressed by him, who regards his languour as an enviable aristocratic virtue, and who will serve him faithfully? In his novel, Goncharov works out for us the answer to this multiple question.

That the result is a great comic story, the world knows. The reader as yet unacquainted with it will discover its pleasures for himself as he turns its pages. He will meet a juicy character, a monstrosity of indolence wrapped in the most famous dressing-gown in the literature of laziness, a man who, as he yawns his way through one evasion after another, is always a magnet for our sympathies as well as for our friendly laughter.

15

Comment on Leavis

F. R. Leavis's *Sewanee Review* comments on my two-volume edition of *The Collected Letters of D. H. Lawrence* were made with the sweetness, tolerance, and Old World courtesy which we have all learned to expect from him. His repetition of the Who-is-Professor-Moore-that-he-should-dare? question focuses attention on the editor rather than on the author of the twelve hundred letters. That this particular editor, with Guggenheim assistance, could bring to light more Lawrence letters than perhaps anyone else is not directly pointed out by Dr. Leavis, but he probably meant to suggest it when he wrote, with such magnanimity and grace, "Professor Moore takes over Lawrence as an established classic on whom he has been able to consolidate his own position as an 'authority' with immediate academic credit and munificent institutional support." As files of American magazines will show, I was publicly supporting Lawrence in the 1930s and 40s when he was emphatically unfashionable and far from being "an established classic." That Dr. Leavis should be unaware of such points of Lawrence scholarship is pardonable, for over the years he has been fruitfully occupied in constructing for his Cambridge parishioners an image of their minister as a figure of neglected greatness.

Dr. Leavis, whose reputation for accuracy is not exactly

"Correspondence." *Sewanee Review*, Spring 1963. Reprinted with permission of the *Sewanee Review*. Copyright 1963 by The University of the South.

remarkable, charitably mentions some errors in the Lawrence *Letters*. These will of course be corrected in later editions. Their occurrence is partly attributable to a printers'
delay in sending proofs on schedule, at a time when I was
free to work on them, with necessary books and papers at
hand; the proofs had to be read, in haste because of the delay, when I was away from my source material and when my
time was by contract heavily committed to other activities.
Naturally Dr. Leavis couldn't know all this, earnestly
engaged as he was in elevating the tone of humane studies
by instructing his followers to use literary criticism as the
nobly idealistic Storm Troopers, gaily singing the "Horst
Wessel Lied," used rubber truncheons on the skulls of
those who disagreed with them.

Most of Dr. Leavis's concern in the *Sewanee Review* was
with such topics as Lawrence's temperament, *roman à clef*
identifications, the film of *Sons and Lovers*, Middleton
Murry's critical abilities, and other such matters that di-
verted attention from those twelve hundred Lawrence letters
which offer the conscientious reviewer abundant opportu-
nity for creative interpretation. In treating all those incidental matters with his habitually courteous respect for
other points of view, Dr. Leavis with perhaps unconscious
altruism confirmed the findings on him by a young critic,
George Watson (in *The Literary Critics*, Penguin, 1962),
who saw him as one vehement out of all proportion, one
"whose absolute refusal to admit honest errors of judgment
sapped the confidence of some of his most serious admirers."
Just as well that such weaklings should break away: down
with tolerance of other points of view and up with the savage
absolutes of dogmatism!

Regrettably, there isn't space to quote some of the letters
which have come in since Dr. Leavis's latest outburst of
benevolence; they would indicate what some younger writers and teachers think of such displays. But let's not take
Dr. Leavis's attention away from his good works any
longer. I'll end on a compassionate note by citing a phrase
William Gerhardie recently applied to him in the *Spectator* in one of the many similar letters that journal received

after exposing its readers to the blaze of sweetness and light which Dr. Leavis had turned upon C. P. Snow. The shrewdly witty Mr. Gerhardie, in pointing out that Dr. Leavis had manifested *la folie des grandeurs*, has made it possible for us to leave the subject with a sympathetic insight which explains Dr. Leavis's recent activities.

16

Dreiser and the Inappropriate Biographer

"The feet of Theodore are making a path, the heavy brutal feet"—as Sherwood Anderson wrote in a prose poem whose own crudeness suggests the clumsy strength of Theodore Dreiser at the time Dreiser was writing his novels and in his plodding way helping to forward the cause of realism in American fiction.

W. A. Swanberg's biography of Dreiser (1871–1945) is the first full one. Its equally scholarly but considerably briefer predecessor, by Robert H. Elias, dates from 1948, when the second Mrs. Dreiser was still alive; and Elias was properly discreet. Helen Dreiser died ten years ago, so Swanberg can tell all now. He does.

Dreiser himself wrote rather bluntly of his early years in autobiographical books such as *Dawn* and *Newspaper Days*, but just how wretched his middle-western youth really was never has been stressed so emphatically as in the present volume. His father was a stern, German-born Catholic, his mother a woman of "pagan" inclination.

The family lived in dismal poverty, and the shy, gawky boy was humiliated by the amorous escapades of his older sisters, though after he grew up he had no scruples about using their affairs for literary copy in his novels, *Sister Carrie* and *Jennie Gerhardt*. He partly admired and partly envied the success of his brother Paul, who changed his last name to Dresser and became an actor and song writer.

Dreiser. By W. A. Swanberg. Charles Scribner's Sons. (*Chicago Tribune Books Today*, April 25, 1965. Reprinted by permission.)

After some years as a reporter in Chicago, St. Louis, and Pittsburgh, Theodore Dreiser joined his brother in New York. There he wrote the words for "On the Banks of the Wabash," to Paul's music. Today their home town of Terre Haute, Indiana, displays a plaque celebrating Paul, whose greatest success was that tinny song, "My Gal Sal"; but the local chamber of commerce has done nothing to commemorate Theodore, author of several novels whose importance is established in the modern literary canon.

From the first, Dreiser had troubles with publishers and censors. Ironically, he was for several years editor of a fashionable woman's magazine. That career ended abruptly with a scandal in 1910 and, for the rest of his life, Dreiser teetered between poverty and comparative wealth. After *An American Tragedy* in 1925, he wrote no more novels that were to be published during his lifetime. Instead, he fooled around rather pompously trying to be a sage, attempting to comment on philosophy, science, and politics, quarreling frequently with H. L. Mencken and other friends. Above all, Dreiser devoted an almost fabulous amount of time to women.

It would be fabulous indeed if the present book didn't document the love affairs so exhaustively. The huge, buck-toothed, craggy-faced Dreiser was a magnet for women young and old. They usually reported that he was a kind man, though he certainly treated his first wife callously. As for the second, he kept her dangling for a quarter-century before marrying her. Meanwhile, he paraded other girls before her, and she sometimes had to serve them breakfast.

A certain amount of philandering might be expected from a small-town boy dazzled by international fame, but Dreiser's love affairs were, to use a comparatively mild word, excessive. The evidence of this painstakingly annotated book can only convince the reader that in his daily life Dreiser was a megalomaniac Don Juan.

And the book will assuredly tend to reduce the stature of Dreiser the author. Too many people are, in Oscar Wilde's phrase, incapable of separating the art from the artist. This volume will demonstrate once again, to those of us who believe literary biography can be valid, that this kind of book is best written by a seasoned literary critic.

As an example of what can be accomplished along that line, consider Richard Ellmann's *James Joyce*, which examined the life of Joyce as thoroughly as it could be done, in the spirit of Oliver Cromwell's advice to a man painting his portrait, whom he told to include warts and all in the picture. Yet Ellmann's book, for all its stark candor about Joyce, makes illuminating comments on his imaginative work.

In the Dreiser biography, Swanberg merely provides bare synopses of some of the principal novels and quotes a few reviews and general opinions about them. He never gets down to showing why Dreiser is a significant author, particularly in such books as *Sister Carrie* and *An American Tragedy*.

Granted, Dreiser is not a writer of the magnitude of Joyce, but in spite of its obvious faults, his work is valuable, and for more than the historic reason that he was a courageous pioneer. An informed artistic defense of him would show him as less of a beast than this elaborate recording of his life makes him out to be. Further, a literary critic might have been able to give a proper assessment of Dreiser's manifest stupidities and to have shown that in his novels he often revealed the instinctive art-wisdom of the authentic creator, something that didn't carry over into his efforts at abstract thinking.

It is necessary at this point to say that W. A. Swanberg is an excellent biographer when he has an appropriate subject. The men he dealt with so successfully in previous books — General Sickles, Jim Fisk, W. R. Hearst — were not artists. Swanberg knows recent American history expertly, he is a tirelessly accurate researcher, and he has the true biographer's knack of keeping his eye on the subject, of not letting the weight of factual material draw him away from the human aspects of his subject. But, in dealing with an artist, he simply is out of his range.

Even though Swanberg may be essentially sympathetic to

the often-blundering Hoosier he writes of here, Dreiser comes out of these pages a monster, and in their context he is a monster. But he deserves a hearing on behalf of his genuine accomplishment, the kind of hearing that a literary critic writing a biography of Dreiser would have given him.

17

Simenon's Artist-Saint
of the rue Mouffetard

The Belgian-born French writer Georges Simenon is best
known in the United States for his novels about Inspector
Maigret, who has been the favorite sleuth of highbrow
detective-story readers since Dorothy L. Sayers's Lord Peter
Wimsey ceased functioning in the 1930s. The latest count
shows that Simenon has written about seventy Maigret
books, and more than three hundred and fifty other works
of fiction published under pseudonyms. But he has also
produced about one hundred and eighty "serious" novels,
many of which have won him high praise in Europe. André
Gide went so far as to place Simenon in the front rank of
modern French authors.

The Little Saint may be the most joyous novel Simenon
has written; he says that in the present volume he was able
to create for the first time "a perfectly serene character, in
immediate contact with nature and life."

Most of Simenon's novels are unrelievedly grim, even the
ones penetrated by Maigret's wry humor. Among those
classified as serious, *Sunday* is typical: it is the tense story of
a chef in a small Riviera hotel owned by his unsympathetic
wife, whom he tries to poison, thus bringing about a disaster he hadn't counted on. In *The Snow Was Black*, a young
man in an unnamed country which is in the grip of a Nazi-
like army murders one of the occupation troops and is

The Little Saint. By Georges Simenon. Harcourt, Brace, and World.
(*Saturday Review*, October 30, 1965. Copyright 1965 by Saturday Review, Inc. Reprinted by permission.)

caught and executed. The autobiographical *Pedigree* deals with a child and his family living in comparative poverty in Liège. *Striptease* bares the odious lives of cabaret girls in Cannes. And so it goes. Even *The Little Saint* has its quota of sordidness.

The title comes from the name given by his schoolmates to the central character, who is not actually a saint. But Louis does have some of the attributes that make consecrated people so difficult to have around in everyday life. For one thing, he is genuinely meek. He has no capacity for dislike; if the schoolyard bully demands Louis's colored marbles, he gives them up ungrudgingly. This of course evokes general mockery and distrust. As Louis grows older he becomes somewhat adjusted to life and overcomes various handicaps, including a sexual shyness induced by the domestic circumstances of his early childhood. He goes to work at the sprawling Paris market, Les Halles; and then he discovers an activity that interests, indeed consumes him, taking him away at last from the great sheds where the city's food is sold.

Most of the book concentrates on Louis's childhood and adolescence in the 1890s and the early years of this century. With brothers and sisters of various ages, he inhabits a tenement room in which the children are all too acutely aware of their mother's nightly jousts of love in the adjoining cell. Some men appear only briefly, others stay awhile. There had been a husband, but he drowned himself. The children aren't sure which of them might be legitimate, or even which of the visiting men might have been their fathers.

Here is an authentically grimy picture of life as it buzzes on in the midst of an ancient city, in the streets behind the palaces, boulevards, and gardens which the tourists know. The principal setting is the narrow and grubby rue Mouffetard, a bit to the southeast of the domed Panthéon, where some of France's heroes are enshrined. The rue Mouffetard existed in Villon's cramped little Paris; it bristled with Jacobins in the eighteenth century, and in our own time Hemingway has graphically described it. Simenon, in his inti-

mate views of the life there, doesn't omit squalid details.
In that little space in which Louis grows up the family
chamber-pot plays a hideously emphatic rôle, and the pu-
bescent perversions that flourish in the children's room
would provide some bizarre passages for a future Krafft-
Ebing or Kinsey researcher.

Yet the mother of the children is, in her feline way, a
devoted one. Often she gets up as early as three in the
morning to trudge across the Seine to Les Halles, pushing a
cart which she fills with vegetables to sell in the rackety
street-markets of her own district. At dusk she always brings
home good food for the children. Simenon, too, has a
tender concern for them. As they grow up he follows
them out into the larger world and periodically reports on
their later lives, which for the most part all too cruelly reflect their smudged beginnings. But Louis toughly survives
in that environment, and if his meekness is one saintly
quality, he has another in his love for all of life.

The early parts of the story prepare us for his sudden
metamorphosis into a painter. In childhood, Louis con-
stantly discovers "images, yellow and green house fronts,
signboards, nooks crowded with barrels." Visiting Les Halles
with his mother, the boy tells her to buy a certain assort-
ment of apples because they are cheap and are the red kind
children like; he doesn't "add that he admired the crimson
color of the pippins, the golden, star-shaped designs that
illuminated their skin, their slightly flattened shape." Louis
at last teaches himself to paint, and to do so in his own
way, fumbling toward his essential vision. Simenon himself,
it might be noted, has always been particularly interested in
the early twentieth-century painters known as the *Fauves*
("Wild Beasts"). He conveys in a few deft word-strokes the
effect of Louis's savagely individualistic painting, which
ostensibly brings him fame almost within the shadow of the
Panthéon.

The last part of his career, his progress into manhood and
artistry, is rather hastily and at times vaguely sketched in.
Too many of Simenon's books crumble toward the end or
close with a jolting abruptness. But this one, like a great

number of the others, deserves the reader's gratitude if only for the current of life that vibrates so wonderfully through most of the story. The character of Louis is touchingly attractive, and if he is at one level alienated from the community as a special man, he is at other levels not apart from it because he is an intensification of what is good in the community. His story is at once lively, realistic, genial, and magnetic.

18
_____

Some Notes
on John Steinbeck's Later Works

As indicated in the foreword to this second edition of *The Novels of John Steinbeck*, the awarding of the Nobel Prize for Literature to Steinbeck in 1962 met with general disapproval. (Though we may wonder where all the carpers were when Pearl Buck received the prize, which long since should have gone to Lewis Mumford, Thornton Wilder, or even to the late Robert Frost.) Since 1939, when the present book first appeared at the same time as *The Grapes of Wrath*, Steinback's career has proved to be a disappointment to those who have wanted to admire him without losing their critical values. Consider such quackery as *The Pearl* ("This Pearl is like a sin! It will destroy us."), of which a blurb writer blurted out, "Only John Steinbeck could write a book like this!"—alas, all too true.

This epilogue will deal only briefly with Steinbeck's later works. It is drawn to some extent from two of my reviews: from the *New Republic* of May 27, 1957, and from *American Literature* of November 1958. The first of these pieces was a discussion of one of Steinbeck's later novels, *The Short Reign of Pippin IV: A Fabrication* (Viking Press), and of *Steinbeck and his Critics: an Anthology and Notes* (University of New Mexico Press), edited by E. W. Tedlock, Jr., and C. V. Wicker. The second review, the one in *American Literature*, dealt with Peter Lisca's *The*

"Epilogue" in second (1968) edition of *The Novels of John Steinbeck*. (Copyright 1939 by Normanidie House; Copyright 1968 by Harry T. Moore. Reprinted by permission of Kennikat Press.)

Wide World of John Steinbeck (Rutgers University Press).

The *New Republic* article on the Tedlock-Wicker anthology and on *Pippin IV* began by saying that now and then the bloated literary reputations need to be punctured. Admittedly, it's less fun to jab away at Steinbeck than at some of the other overinflated authors, for he has consistently and ardently been the champion of causes of which seasoned liberals approve; and those professionally concerned with literature today are, almost invariably, seasoned liberals. But it takes more than sponsorship of good causes to make a man a novelist of the stature claimed for Steinbeck in the Tedlock-Wicker anthology of "critical" bouquets, which should properly have been called *Steinbeck and his Worshippers.*

The reason so many of Steinbeck's former admirers no longer enjoy his work is that the weaknesses of the earlier writings, excusable enough in a young novelist, have prevailed: the woodenness and the sentimentalism. Over the years he has become the idol of book clubs and movie audiences, and of a vast uninstructed reading public. Literary experts of high standing have either ignored Steinbeck or, in critical books and journals of limited circulation, have exposed his defects. Edmund Wilson, Alfred Kazin, and Maxwell Geismar are three important critics, for example, who have detailed Steinbeck's imperfections: ironically, in an anthology whose title implies criticism, the comments of these three experts do not appear amid the flourish of uncritical tributes.

Consider one case from *Steinbeck and his Critics.* Martin Staples Shockley, in his essay on "Christian Symbolism in *The Grapes of Wrath,*" takes up a great deal of space trying to show that Jim Casy, the itinerant preacher in that novel, is a Christ symbol. This is nothing new: readers of *The Grapes of Wrath* when it came out in 1939 readily enough saw the connection between such statements as Christ's "Father, forgive them; for they know not what they do" and Casy's "You fellas don' know what you're doin'"—the latter not referring to the soldiers of Tiberius but to California vigilantes wearing American Legion caps and about to knock Casy's brains out with a pick-handle. The trouble is that our searcher of texts fails to see, or at least fails to mention, that this is really not significant parallel, but crude parody.

Similarly, in the scene in which the Joads' daughter Rosasharn breast-feeds the starving old man, Shockley finds this bit of Maupassant-like naturalism an example of "the ultimate mystery of the Christian religion." For, "in this, her Gethsemane, Rosasharn says, in effect, 'Not my will but Thine be done.'" The "in effect" saves Steinbeck—to some extent. He of course makes frequent use of myth and symbol, though not always so preposterously as some of his latest admirers seem to think he does. But he serves up enough bogus writing to encourage these extravagant responses—surely they must embarrass him?

Of course posterity, capricious posterity, may accept Steinbeck as another Tolstoy; but surely this is doubtful, not credible at all in view of today's high-level critical opinion—the kind of opinion missing from *Steinbeck and his Critics*. As for the professionals, Steinbeck scorns them, or so he protests in several articles scattered across that anthology. Sometimes he crosses himself up, as in his polemical "Critics, Critics, Burning Bright," written for the *Saturday Review* in 1950 after the New York aisle-sitters had expressed disapproval of his play, *Burning Bright*. Perhaps his assurance that he is "not criticizing critics" is meant to be ironic, for he speaks of most of those who disliked his drama as emotional, hysterical, and vehement; they were so enraged at the unusual idiom of the play that "they did not investigate the theme." It is confusing to come across this essay toward the middle of the Tedlock-Wicker anthology; earlier in the book, the reader has been told, in Peter Lisca's biographical chapter—apparently checked by Steinbeck himself—that

four years after the book's publication [Steinbeck] admitted in private conversation that the play was a failure in writing, that it was too abstract, that it preached too much, and that the audience was always a step ahead of it.

And how many steps ahead, one can only wonder, were those bright-burning critics?

One word more on this *hommage* volume; on its last page, Steinbeck in a single sentence reveals why he writes with such sentimentalism and embarrassing naïveté. It almost seems as if he wished he could meet his own Preacher Casy, who said, "I love people so much I'm fit to bust sometimes." Of himself, Steinbeck writes on that blushing last page, "like everyone, I want to be good and strong and virtuous and wise and loved."

And there you have it. There you also have the reason why Steinbeck shouldn't attempt satire—which is what both he and the blurb writer call his *Pippin IV* novel. Actually, it is a gentle little comedy, superficially amusing for a while; but long before its 188th and final page, it begins to pall.

For this *Pippin* story is no more than an extended anecdote about a king who tries to be more democratic than the democrats and thereby gets into trouble of a traditional French-revolutionary kind. The fable is a cliché, and most of its language is cliché masquerading as epigram: "There's no snob like a self-made man," and so on. Throughout, the characters are made to speak like those in a phrase book. The king appears to be likeable enough, and his relatives try to be. There is for example the uncle who deals in proverbs and fake paintings, whom the author has, appropriately enough, contrived with painful fakery; and there is the king's daughter, a recognizable cartoon of a teen-age French novelist, almost as profoundly created as the takeoffs, on television shows, of well-known people. Odd: American writers used to "do" Europeans so well, comically or otherwise, between the times of Washington Irving and Henry James; in American fiction today, only Kay Boyle has presented convincing Europeans.

As for satire itself, surely Steinbeck is too softhearted for the medium, for which Swift's *saeve indignatio* is needed; or at least the chill upper lip of Evelyn Waugh. In this category, a squashy sentimentalism becomes merely a squashy sentimentalism. Nevertheless, the continuing admirers of Steinbeck—the book-club members and movie worshippers—

will probably consider this novel an important mutation in his career and will nourish the book with the usual over-praise.

Of course *Pippin IV* received the accolade of the Book-of-the-Month Club, though professional critics granted it little, if indeed they paid any attention to it at all. Discussion of *Pippin* in that 1957 *New Republic* review was incidental to the consideration of the Tedlock-Wicker anthology, which ignored the important critics mentioned above (Wilson, Kazin, Geismar) for floral (and florid) tributes. One of that book's misdemeanors is its paraphrasing of Mark Schorer's praise of *East of Eden* (1952) in the *New York Times Book Review*. The editors of *Steinbeck and his Critics* had asked Mark Schorer if they could have permission to reprint that review in their book. Permission was firmly denied, according to Peter Lisca in his later volume on Steinbeck; Schorer had written to one of the editors of the anthology, C. V. Wicker, in 1955, saying that after re-reading the novel he had (according to Lisca) "found the review totally mistaken in judgment and regretted its publication." This did not, however, prevent *Steinbeck and his Critics* from citing the opinions expressed in that review as if Mark Schorer still held them.

Mr. Lisca's own volume, *The Wide World of John Steinbeck* (1958), is a book-by-book analysis of the writings of John Steinbeck which compels admiration for its industry, but not necessarily for all its judgments. One of Lisca's principal themes is that serious critics have unduly neglected Steinbeck since the 1930s, when he first landed on the best-seller lists with his stories of naïvely comic primitives and the "forgotten man" of New Deal speeches. In those days Steinbeck, who avoided Marxist "agitprop" extremes, certainly wrote better novels than the members of the marching-marching, make-my-bread, hammer-and-anvil school. That Steinbeck, like so many other American authors, failed to grow with success is another of Mr. Lisca's important points. But he places this arrest of maturity fairly late in Steinbeck's career: after *The Wayward Bus* (1947). To critics such as the previously mentioned Geismar, Kazin, and Wilson, as well as to Leslie Fiedler (who viewed the awarding of the Nobel Prize to Steinbeck as "ironic"), the late Frederick J. Hoffman, the late James Thurber, and others, signs of the deficiency in growth had been apparent long before.

By 1939 the mechanical and rhetorical aspects of *The Grapes of Wrath*, which across the years has remained Steinbeck's most widely respected book, indicated that he was not developing the promise of his earlier novels. These had suggested that in time Steinbeck might project a vision of the natural world comparable in quality to that of some of the better European writers, and that he might improve his ability to dramatize man's conflict with either an implacable fate or destructive social forces. But *The Grapes of Wrath* suffered from the weaknesses of the previous work: the rigidity of prose and fable, and the tendency of the author's generous emotional impulses to become mawkish.

In his defense of *The Grapes of Wrath*, Mr. Lisca emphasizes its structure and evokes Tolstoy and the Greeks. But the story itself escapes Mr. Lisca's attempts to play down the importance of its human agents who, although they do not act but are acted upon, cannot be easily minimized, incredible as they often seem. Steinbeck's universal-individual family of Joads behave as if they knew Maupassant and speak as if they read Sandburg: these artifically simple folk become increasingly unbelievable the more they intellectualize their position as "the people," who are "goin' right on." As noted earlier, the Joads' friend Casy is certainly a Christ-figure, and Mr. Lisca points this out, also uncritically; he further sees Casy as a manifestation of Emerson's Oversoul. All this is somewhat similar to certain mawkishly mystical phases of the later Hemingway and Faulkner and of some of their worshipful interpreters: what is meant to be, or is at least suspected of being religiously, philosophically, and artistically impressive too often turns out to be embarrassingly parodic.

A number of the critics who in 1939 had swallowed *The Grapes of Wrath* found themselves, three years later, straining at *The Moon is Down*. Here a "German" officer spoke, through the stiffness of plot and character, lines that seemed a bewildering lampoon of Conrad Aiken ("I like the sweet, cool smell of the snow," he says more than once). And even if the story was written with an honest sympathy for victims of oppression, the propagandist tone imposed its own oppressiveness. Nevertheless, a number of reviewers liked *The Moon is Down.* In summing up the conflicting responses, Mr. Lisca points out that "the King of Norway thought enough of its effectiveness to decorate Steinbeck for it [*sic*]"—a statement that hardly clinches the argument, artistically, for the affirmative. That Mr. Lisca, despite Steinbeck's having received the accolades of reviewers and royalty, eventually became disillusioned with his work ("after 1947") is not surprising. Steinbeck does not wear well. Older critics perhaps made the break earlier because they had come to Steinbeck earlier than Peter Lisca.

In his scholarship, Mr. Lisca is accurate and resourceful. He has even coaxed biographical details out of a reticent author, most of them concerning his methods of work, here often described by Steinbeck himself in previously unprinted letters to his publishers and agents. And while all this is interesting and valuable, Mr. Lisca's book must be measured at the last by its *critical* validity: is Steinbeck worth all this solemn consideration—and if not, just how much of it *is* he worth? As we have seen, a respectable group of Mr. Lisca's predecessors have defined Steinbeck's limitations. Mr. Lisca, in opposing these older critics, often goes to extremes in his estimates of Steinbeck, as when at the end of his discussion of *The Wayward Bus* he seriously implies comparisons to Dante and Swift. Sometimes Mr. Lisca's evaluations are no more than unsupported assertions: what does he mean, for example, when he says that one story "has more reality" than another; and what, even approximately, does "significant form," that oversimple phrase with so many different meanings for so many different people, mean to Peter Lisca? Such matters may not disturb the vast book-club audience that responds to Steinbeck and cares little about critical precision. But generalities and suggested likenesses to authors of established magnitude will hardly change the minds of the critics who have felt, across the years, that Steinbeck has been overrated.

There is little more to be said except to note that John Steinbeck has, since the Lisca volume in 1958, written another novel, *The Winter of Our Discontent* (1961) merely a competent book, and *Travels with Charley* (1962), a genuinely amusing and informative account of the author's cross-country journeys with a dog. The reflective *America and the Americans* came along in 1966. Also, there have been several other "about" books, including Warren French's *John Steinbeck* (1961), in the Twayne United States Authors Series, and Joseph Fontenrose's *John Steinbeck: An Introduction and Interpretation* (1963) in the Barnes and Noble American Authors and Critics Series. Warren French, who in 1963 brought out *A Companion to the Grapes of Wrath* (Viking Press, 1963), an extremely useful background book, overrates Steinbeck—or tries to—in his volume in the Twayne series. He begins by decrying the low critical status of Steinbeck—but critics of the stature of Edmund Wilson are simply not going to accept this author. When Mr. French arrives at the end of his book, all he can say is that there should be a higher place in literary esteem for the man who wrote Steinbeck's novels—and the most this critic can do is list a few of the earlier ones. While Mr. French deals largely with the sociological, Mr. Fontenrose for the most part treats the mythical aspects of Steinbeck's work; both these men make valuable contributions to our knowledge of this writer, but they inflate him to a size that is not rightly his. He is simply not a major figure. Warren French doesn't invoke Dante, as Peter Lisca does, but he joins Mr. Lisca is calling up Shakespeare and Swift for comparisons to an author whose peers, as passing time increasingly shows, are the Louis Bromfields and Bess Streeter Aldriches.

At a time when people were hungry and dispossessed and wandering, Steinbeck was one of their literate spokesmen. But too many readers mistook his sentimentalism for compassion; sentimentalism, that is, in the sense of tearfully expecting too much from life. We can perform a service to our culture, to the preservation of its truest values, by not overrating the work of this man of goodwill who was sometimes a competent novelist, though never "great."

19

Hemingway and a Chronology
without Characterization

Ernest Hemingway conducted so much of his life in public
that he became a legendary figure of Byronic proportions.
And now Professor Carlos Baker of Princeton has written a
full account of that life, scrupulously recording all the facts
connected with it.

Much of the story is well known. There is Hemingway's
Oak Park boyhood in the early years of this century, with
the wonderful Michigan summers whose quality is best suggested by his poetic story, "Big Two-Hearted River." Then
there is World War I, with the very young man sustaining
critical wounds while serving in the Italian ambulance corps.
The Paris years follow, with the youthful newspaperman
slowly building his reputation as a writer of fiction which
has the special stamp of a new kind of prose. Fame comes at
last, with four marriages, and an established pattern of life:
following the bullfights, going deep-sea fishing off Cuba,
and hunting big game in Africa. Then the last fatal act
occurs at the ranch in the Idaho mountains.

It was a sensitive, insecure, and deeply suffering man who
underwent all these experiences. He had an extravagant
zest for life, too, and in his writing and sporting activities
could often forget his anxieties. But his behavior, as recorded
here, was often outrageous. Hemingway had a gift for com-
radeship, but without warning would turn savagely on the

Ernest Hemingway: A Life Story. By Carlos Baker. Charles Scribner's Sons. (*Chicago Daily News,* April 5, 1969. Reprinted with permission from the *Chicago Daily News.*)

closest of his friends. A good part of the time he acted like a spoiled child.

None of this, however, should make us forget Hemingway's achievement as a writer, particularly his first two serious novels, *The Sun Also Rises* and *A Farewell to Arms*, as well as his remarkable short stories, many of the best of them belonging to the early part of his career. In the present book, Mr. Baker does not provide critical commentaries, partly because he published a volume about Hemingway's work several years ago, a valuable study which tended to overrate the later phases of Hemingway's writing career; but in the present book, while not dealing in evaluations, Mr. Baker never lets us forget Hemingway the author. And of course his writings are the central point of the biography, indeed its reason for being. Mr. Baker deals with the origins and development of Hemingway's work, analyzes that author's ideas about it, and discusses the critical and public response to it.

Mr. Baker writes in a good, clear style that never imitates Hemingway's, although in one respect this biographer does follow a Hemingway method. That is, he lets character come through action, simply showing what people did and said and making almost no general comments. We can of course be grateful that Mr. Baker didn't attempt a heavily psychoanalytical biography, though the method he did choose has its own limitations, in that only circumstances and particulars arise from the narrative, and no clear, full picture of the subject emerges.

To mention one point in connection with this statement: what of Hemingway's behavior toward critics who felt that his books were sometimes a bit less than perfect? He wanted to beat them up or fight duels with them. Was he totally serious in this, or partly jesting? Even if the latter were true, is not the manifestation still an unhealthy one? Mr. Baker provides nothing in the way of an answer to such inevitable questions.

In his narration of events, he is sometimes uncomfortably chummy. The continual use of the name Ernest is forgivable, for even though Mr. Baker never met Hemingway it would make his text drag if he repeatedly used the longer surname. But the reader is too cosily nudged into meetings with Ezra, Gertrude, Max, and the others. Leonard Lyons is introduced into the text and is at once tagged Lenny. Everyone in the book with the first name of William immediately becomes Bill. Maybe this is meant to suggest the Hemingway touch, but it is a method used rarely enough in serious biographies to make some readers of this one squirm just a little.

On the positive side, we can appreciate much that Mr. Baker has given us. His accumulation of material was, as he has termed it, "a seven-year siege." Everyone seriously interested in modern literature is in his debt for this book; if it isn't a perfect biography, it is at least a valuable chronicle.

20

John O'Hara Tries the Novel Again

John O'Hara is often a master of the short story, crisp and assured. But when it comes to the novel he is usually lost, even in a fairly brief one such as *Lovey Childs*, which runs to only 249 pages. Too much is slurred over or left undeveloped.

The book, however, contains some excellent scenes. And, as always, O'Hara gives an interestingly accurate picture of a time and place, on this occasion the 1920s and '30s in and around Philadelphia. Lovey is the daughter of a wealthy Main Line horseman who is killed in a riding accident when the girl is sixteen. Not long after this, Lovey's attractive mother is seduced by a girl friend her daughter has brought home from school, after which the mother tries to become a practicing lesbian and winds up insane. All this part of the story is expertly done, and the lesbian scenes are erotically graphic.

Lovey marries a football star, Schuyler ("Sky") Childs, and their life together is summarized in a few pages in which they appear to be a Scott Fitzgerald-like couple in the glittering era. But as for Lovey's possible inner growth, the author gives us nothing, and we never really see her husband (we hear him once on a breaking-off-relations telephone call). Lovey obtains a divorce in Reno, where a female newspaper reporter seduces her. She seems at the moment to be

Lovely Childs: A Philadelphian's Story. By John O'Hara. Random House. (*Chicago Daily News*, December 27–28, 1969. Reprinted with permission from the *Chicago Daily News*.)

won over to lesbianism, but the remainder of the book contains only one casual reference to this experience. The newspaperwoman is apparently not kept on, but the narrative provides no indication that she has been rejected, no parting scene, just nothing.

Also, the author gives us only a quick and superficial introduction to Lovey's second husband and sums up their forty years of marriage in less than two pages at the end of the book. The somewhat wild Lovey settles down to a quiet existence in her native Philadelphia, but just why she does so is never made clear.

As noted earlier, the book has some excellent episodes, attributable to John O'Hara's skill as a writer of short stories. There is, for example, Lovey's brief love affair with a priest, which has fatal consequences. And the incidents surrounding the murder of a man Lovey knows are handled with the notable O'Hara skill. The speech of his characters of all kinds is, as always, most convincing. And although the book lacks the proportionment a novel should have, it often rolls along smoothly. But the reader does miss the principle of development, particularly in relation to the central character.

21

Age of the Modern

The Background of Today's Thought

What is modern in art and literature—or, more specifically, what is twentieth-centuryish? A great deal that is remarkable along traditional lines has been accomplished in this epoch, but there is also much excellent art that breaks away from tradition and catches various phases of the spirit of the epoch itself. What characterizes such art?

Any attempt at an answer will have to take into consideration some backgrounds of that exciting period when Europe was moving toward the First World War.

Politically and morally, the twentieth century didn't begin until the outbreak of that war, but technically and artistically the epoch started some years before the conflict; indeed, close to the time when the calendar said the century began.

The effects of that First World War will be considered later, after some glances at the background of modern thought. How did twentieth-century man, who among other activities produces and reads twentieth-century literature, become what he is, intellectually?

The Polish monk Copernicus, who died in 1543, is one starting point toward an answer. Before Copernicus's time, most western men had lived through a thousand years of believing one thing about the structure of the universe: they accepted the ancient Ptolemaic concept that the sun moved around the earth. As long as men subscribed to this

Previously unpublished; revised 1970.

idea, they saw the world as the central stage of the universe for the acting out of the drama of good and evil whereby they prepared themselves for the heaven or hell of the after-life.

Realizing the revolutionary possibilities of his own oppos-ing theories of a sun-centered universe, Copernicus delayed their publication; when they were at last printed in the year he died, little attention was paid to them. But by 1616, seventy-three years later, the Church had recognized their threat and put them on the Index. Galileo, basing some of his experiments on the Copernican discoveries, was in 1633 forced by the Inquisition to renounce them (though legend says that, as Galileo left the torture chamber, he muttered that the ideas he had declared to be false were nevertheless true). Later, in Protestant England, Sir Isaac Newton (1642–1727) could safely work out his theories of gravity, optics, and other matters, using the science which had developed from Copernicus and others.

By this time, most men had ceased to think of an earth-centered universe and were more concerned with present material contentment than they had been in the Catholic Middle Ages. And although Luther among early Protes-tants attacked the theories of Copernicus, they fitted in neatly with the exploration and exploitation of new conti-nents and, on the economic side, with what the German economic philosopher Max Weber was later to call the prot-estant ethic in *Die protestantische Ethik und der Geist des Kapitalismus*, (1904–5; *The Protestant Ethic and the Spirit of Capitalism*). Luther preached the holiness of work for profit, and Calvin intensified this idea. The middle ages stig-matized interest as usury, not a Christian practice, but now the rising Protestants, particularly the Calvinist groups and their offshoots known as the Puritans, celebrated thrift in the kingdom of this world to which Copernicus had first em-phatically called attention. Later, it was the capital nurtured in the Calvinist countries which helped finance the Indus-trial Revolution.

Meanwhile, another line of belief had developed, again made possible by Copernicus: what may be thought of in general as naturalism in the theories of Jean-Jacques Rousseau, Charles Darwin, Karl Marx, and Sigmund Freud (naturalism, that is, in that the doctrines of these men ultimately led away from the supernatural). The second of these moulders of modern thought, Darwin, was a scientist, and the fourth of them, Freud, is usually considered so; the work of the quartet is capped by that genuine and extraordinary scientist, Albert Einstein. Some philosophers also fit into the picture, among them René Descartes, Immanuel Kant, Georg Wilhelm Friedrich Hegel and, in a quite different way, Friedrich Nietzsche.

However widely these men have been read or not read, their thoughts have penetrated the thoughts of all of us and have often influenced the events that have influenced us.

In the early seventeenth century, Descartes, for example, in insisting upon the self as existing because it is conscious, really discovered our concept of "consciousness," expanded by Kant in the eighteenth century and by Hegel in the nineteenth.

These philosophers of consciousness became influences through the minority which was able to read them; the Swiss-French author Jean-Jacques Rousseau had a more direct influence because his writings were immensely popular. Rousseau contributed importantly to the breakup of the eighteenth-century rigidity of systems of belief and behavior, and helped lead toward the French Revolution and the Romantic movement.

Rousseau's career really began on an October day of 1749 when he was on his way to Vincennes to see his friend, the encyclopedist Denis Diderot, who was imprisoned there for having violated an act of censorship. Rousseau had taken with him a copy of the *Mercure de France* to read enroute. In its pages he discovered a notice which, he later said, made him see another universe and become another man. We have all felt the impact of that October afternoon.

The native of Geneva read in the *Mercure* a note to the effect that the Academy of Dijon was offering a prize for a dissertation on the subject, "Has the progress of the arts and sciences tended to the purification or to the corruption of morality?" Rousseau's prizewinning essay elaborated an emphatic demonstration to the effect that "progress" had corrupted morality.

A loose, excited, and often incoherent essay, it nevertheless gave the first indication of Rousseau's force. In *Émile* (1762), he celebrated the natural man in a sermon on education disguised as fiction, in which he attempted to show how a child could be educated within society and yet remain to a certain extent the "noble savage." Rousseau was worshipping an earlier ideal that had come in with the discovery of the New World, where children of nature were reported to be dwelling happily in the great wilderness. But it was Rousseau who carried the idea to popular extremes; his influence stands behind a good part of modern primitivism in art; and it also stands behind a good deal of outdoor activity in the lives of everyday men and women—hiking, tennis, and particularly sunbathing.

In 1762, the year of *Émile*—and actually a few weeks earlier—Rousseau's *Le Contrat Social* (*The Social Contract*) was published. This began with the famous statement, "Man is born free, and everywhere he is in chains." Man lost his freedom, the book goes on to say, when he gave up the state of nature for civilization. Rousseau's solution to the problem is a social contract embodying the "general will" and making no provision for minority rights; a man trying to exercise his "individual will" would have to be constrained—or, as Rousseau puts it, "forced to be free." In these ambiguities we can find the seeds both of democracy, which Rousseau thought he believed in, and of totalitarianism and its compulsions, a nightmare he didn't actually experience. In this dichotomy in Rousseau between freedom and authority, we have in a sense the schizoid constant of the Romantic movement as well as the conflict which the twentieth-century philosopher, Alfred North Whitehead, observed to exist between contemporary man's irrationality and his bondage to determinism.

Rousseau was a man of feeling, as we discover in his romantic novel, *La Nouvelle Héloïse* (*The New Héloïse*); published in 1761, it was the equivalent of a best seller of today. Likewise, in his posthumously published *Confessions* (1781–88), Rousseau emphasized the emotional nature of experience in an embarrassingly candid self-portrait that went a long way toward breaking down eighteenth-century ideals of decorum. Quite as much as Blake and various other neo-Romantics, Rousseau is the father of the Romantic movement, which placed so much emphasis on feeling.

On the side of political influence, Rousseau is teamed with a rationalist and satirist in many ways his opposite—François Marie Arouet de Voltaire—who with him helped bring about the French Revolution of 1789. *Helped bring it about:* the word *helped* is necessary here, for many other forces were at work which also contributed to the explosion of events in 1789 and later. Yet Voltaire and Rousseau, both of whom died eleven years before 1789, had disciples in the French Revolution whose very slogan, "liberty, equality, and fraternity," came out of *The Social Contract.* And to people of the time it certainly seemed that Rousseau and Voltaire were instrumental in bringing about the revolution, for when Louis XVI was in the Bastille he said that those two writers had put him there. French popular wit of the time likewise assigned the "blame" for the revolution—

> *C'est la faute à Voltaire.*
> *C'est la faute à Rousseau.*
> (Voltaire's to blame.
> Rousseau's to blame.)

But enough of Rousseau and his influence, except to note by way of summary that, whatever his effect upon modern politics, he contributed importantly to the Romantic movement, which in many ways is still with us, and to the development of the kind of naturalism which made response to Darwin possible against Victorian opposition. The permeation of the human mind by Rousseau's ideas helped condition it to the concept of the natural man, who could reasonably be descended from a species of primate, and who could also be the possessor of the unconscious which Freud discovered, or at least charted. Indirectly, *The Social Contract* helped make possible the acceptance of Marxism, which was in part built upon the dialectic of another of the philosophers mentioned earlier—Hegel.

Once again, there is necessarily a great deal of simplification here, but amid much complexity in the development of modern thinking, these men who have been mentioned, and their works are among those which stand out prominently. In the century after Rousseau, Darwin explained the physical basis of our existence, (though for one of the recent critical analyses of Darwin's limitations, see Robert Ardrey's *African Genesis*, 1961). As for Marx, however greatly readers may disagree with his advocacy of the need for a dictatorship of the proletariat, they must admit that he was intensely influential in the history of modern thought and of almost all modern governmental activity in that he vigorously called attention to the importance of the economic elements in the life of every nation.

Einstein, inheritor of the scientific tradition, brought to modern man a new world or even universe of physical forces, among other things represented by the all-dominating nuclear bomb which grew out of one of his equations examining the essence of time. Einstein worked out this equation at the beginning of the century, long before the bomb was invented, and also some years before the novel that can be called strictly modernistic began; and what is its beginning if not the stories in Gertrude Stein's *Three Lives* in 1908? (It must be noted that, since her Radcliffe days in the 1890s, Gertrude Stein had been an experimental writer, and that although her big novel *The Making of Americans* was not published until 1925, it was written some seventeen years earlier.) Miss Stein's sentences, which arrested language in mid-flight, were implicitly concerned with time, as so much recent literature is: consider the examinations of time in Thomas Mann's *Der Zauberberg* (1924; *The Magic Mountain*) and in his *Joseph* novels, in James Joyce's fiction, and in Marcel Proust's elongated novel *À la Recherche de temps perdu* (1913–27; *Remembrance of Things Past*), which bears the word *time* in its French title; and in so many other modern works. This is not to say that these authors were devoted followers of Einstein or that they comprehended his theories or even attempted to; but their absorption with time, like Einstein's own, is a signal of their modernness. Time had, as it were, come to a head after centuries of its regulation of and dominance over life, beginning (as Lewis Mumford brilliantly shows in *Technics and Civilization*) with the regimentation of life in the monasteries, whose bells ringing at set intervals gave people in the nearby towns a standard by which to measure their activity —leading among other things to our present condition of life-by-schedule.

The Power of Freud

Perhaps no influence on modern literature has been so direct as that of Freud. Two books which have made a careful study of this influence are Frederick J. Hoffman's *Freudianism and the Literary Mind* (whose revised edition appeared in 1957), which investigates the effect of Freud upon Mann, Joyce, and other authors; and Louis Fraiberg's *Psychoanalysis and American Literary Criticism* (1960), which shows how Van Wyck Brooks, Joseph Wood Krutch, and other American critics have often misapplied Freudian theories. Freud, beginning his work late in the nineteenth century, formulated what the creative giants of literature had known without formulation, and indeed many of his examples of human behavior are taken from the plays of Shakespeare or the novels of Dostoevsky, whose characters Freud treats as if they were actual human beings, case histories out of his own files. But Freud also drew upon numerous actual case histories from his Viennese clinical practice. The therapeutic side of psychoanalysis, really its *raison d'être*, need not concern us here; rather, what is of interest to the study of twentieth-century literature is what Freud discovered enroute to therapy.

First of all, there was his detection of the unconscious, that dark power which lies beyond the range of our immediate awareness but is closely related to it; which festers with the never-quite-lost experiences that begin with birth, the most unpleasant of which are seemingly forgotten but wait for an associative shock to bring them to memory; or, as often happens, these hidden events of the "soul"—the unpleasant experiences, the traumatic or wounding ones—set to work establishing some "complex" or creating a neurosis.

Further, Freud attacked the ancient theory that dreams were prophetic (unless of course the unconscious had directed them toward a probable occurrence); rather, Freud showed that dreams were churned up from the unconscious, either when the memory of some supposedly forgotten experience slipped into the sleeping mind or when pressure of anxiety brought a past or expected shock into the cinema of the brain.

Freud subsequently developed his theories of a tripartite consciousness made up of the Id, the instinctual and unconscious element in the personality; the Ego, the (mostly conscious) organizer of experience and controller of the Id; and the Superego, the parental and traditional aspect of the personality, representing conscience and, usually, conservative authority over the self. The Id is associated with the pleasure principle, which was from the first an important Freudian concern; the Ego is really the mediator between the Id and the Superego; and the Superego represents the moral and social imperatives of the community.

All this has to be drastically simplified here; for fullest comprehension it needs case-history examples and Freud's complicated qualifications; but it is at least a basic explanation of much that appears, deliberately or through unrecognized influence, in modern literature. Further, the present references to these doctrines may lead the reader unfamiliar with Freud into an acquaintanceship with his works, of which a partial understanding is requisite for a thorough knowledge of twentieth-century literature.

Two early followers of Freud, who broke away from his leadership, have also had some influence on the imaginative writings of our time: Alfred Adler and Carl G. Jung. Adler, whose influence has not endured, at least not obviously, felt that Freud gave too much emphasis to sexual manifestations of the personality. Adler, while retaining some of Freud's doctrine, became leader of the school of Individual Psychology, based somewhat on Nietzsche's will-to-power theories. Adler's movement found human affairs dominated by a compensation impulse known popularly as the inferiority complex (Demosthenes stammered, therefore he drove himself to become an expert orator). Several of Adler's phrases, such as the masculine protest—based on the idea that the feeling of inferiority, of *under-ness*, is feminine—entered the currency of daily conversation, so that even if his philosophy is not so openly celebrated as that of Freud, Adler's ideas have neverthelses had some effect on present-day thinking.

Carl G. Jung has been far more influential. Like Adler, he did not altogether repudiate Freud's theories at the time of the break with him, and like Adler he provided some now-familiar terms, such as introvert and extrovert, meaning the man or woman whose interests are essentially turned inward or outward (an idea extended and modified by the popularizing American sociologists with their concepts of inner-directed and other-directed men). Jung's goal, of course, was to establish the personality balanced between its inner and outer components, the true golden mean of the ancients. Jung also developed his own theories of dream symbolism, and published studies on the mythological content of human experience which have engaged the attention of many writers; further, he had a somewhat mystic strain in his theories of *mana*, or the extraphysical power of "*mana* personalities" who have successfully emerged from the "night sea-journey" into their lower selves to become more successful human beings than the average of mankind. Yet, like Adler, Jung has had less influence on modern writing and on recent thought in general than Freud has had.

Thomas Mann was particularly an admirer of Freud, about whom he wrote several illuminating essays—but almost every major writer of our time (even D. H. Lawrence, who disliked Freud and fought against his dominance) has been one way or another affected by him. (An authority on William Faulkner, Carvel Collins, has presented an ingenious interpretation of Faulkner's *The Sound and the Fury* in which three of the leading male characters are seen as representing the Id, the Ego, and the Superego.)

Slips of the tongue are now known as Freudian slips, and virtually everyone has come to think that what people say "by mistake" is what they really meant to say. Such concepts as accident-proneness are essentially Freudian, and the idea of psychosomatic illnesses—now widely recognized by members of the medical profession, most of whom at first opposed Freud—is also essentially a Freudian concept; indeed it was his interest in psychosomatic cases (and of course his genius in seeing their significance) which kept Freud from becoming just another doctor.

A further influence he has had on the twentieth century, in art as well as in the area of general thinking, is in his emphasis on the sexual. When he began publishing his theories, there was a taboo on references to coitus and its related or aberrently variant functions. The idea that children could have a sex life seemed particularly horrifying, even though everyone who was being horrified had once been a child and knew that what Freud said was the truth. It took the courage and patience of a great man to continue publishing such doctrines in the defiance of all totems and taboos.

An admission that sex is a crucial part of life was not confined to Freud, for there were also Edward Carpenter, Richard von Krafft-Ebing, Havelock Ellis, D. H. Lawrence, and others; but it is certain that Freud's persistence, more than any other single effort, made the existence of the sexual publicly recognized earlier than it otherwise would have been. There is still much unwholesomeness, a great deal of smut, in our civilization, but there is also now a greater ease and frankness, so that by the 1960s *Lady Chatterley's Lover* in its unexpurgated form was legally obtainable in English-speaking countries—except in some provinces which are granaries of quaint ideas. By the 1960s, too, the *nouvelle vogue* of the French films, reaching one of its early high points in the scenes between the naked lovers in *Hiroshima mon amour*, were no longer shocking; and in 1961 the

French religious magazine *Esprit* could devote an oversize issue to the "new religion," *la sexualité*. By the 1970s, however, with such films as the Swedish *I Am Curious (Yellow)*, many wondered whether the new freedom had not gone too far; but it may well have established a balance which could bring about a healthier future.

As for Freud: once again, it is not just in sexual matters that he has been so influential; his true importance lies in his concept of the unconscious, in his suggestions as to the meaning of dreams, and in his ideas about "psychopathology in everyday life" such as the slips of the tongue or the fact that the tune one finds oneself humming has some bearing on a past, often recent, experience or on a present intention. The art of our time, whether by Salvador Dali or James Joyce or a hundred or a thousand others, abounds in Freudian ideas and forms.

So far, many trends have been mentioned as comprising the consciousness of the man and woman of today, who are complex creatures retaining many of the crude, violent emotions of the ancient and medieval worlds, and yet are people refined, on the surface at least, by civilization and in general made more comfortable or more safe by its inventions, which have their own ever-recognized perils. Out of all these conditions, modern man has created—and sometimes read—a literature of complexity and often of greatness, the flowering of these influences which have been mentioned.

Every age, we know, produces a dominating atmosphere, tempo, vision: in order to suggest the possibilities of this concept, it might be pointed out—with great oversimplification—that powdered wig means minuet means rhyming couplet, along with the idea of a Deistic entity who has wound up the clockwork world and detached himself from it. In our own time we are perhaps too close to the manifestations of the age itself to determine which of them will later seem the most characteristic; in many cases the artists have discerned important motifs and trends and put these into their works. One example of this is the influence, already mentioned, of Freud's discoveries concerning mental processes, particularly those relating to the unconscious. As also noted earlier, philosophers such as Descartes and Kant had explored the consciousness in the seventeenth and eighteenth centuries.

Their studies were paralleled at another level by the first serious investigations of the pathological and the insane, which at the moment didn't seem connected, though by the time of Freud the essentially cognitive findings could be included, along with inquiries into the pathological, in the category of "the mental."

In the nineteenth century the so-called psychological novel was developed, particularly—toward the end of that period—by Henry James, whose brother William had out of his psychological investigations evolved the concept of stream of thought, which to subsequent imaginative writers became stream of consciousness. Meanwhile, also in the late nineteenth century, such doctors as Jean Martin Charcot and Pierre Janet in Paris and Josef Breuer in Vienna were making studies of hysteria, hypnotism, and other phases of the consciousness. Freud knew Charcot in Paris in the 1880s and even translated his lectures; he had the benefit of critical acquaintance with the theories of Charcot's associate, Janet, but rejected them; and Freud worked with Breuer in Vienna, with whom he eventually broke.

Freud always subsequently gave Breuer great credit for his rôle in the origin of psychoanalysis, but it was Freud, the younger man, who was the true pioneer, the one who carried the work forward while Breuer cautiously hung back. Freud in the 1890s published a book with Breuer which investigated hysteria, but his own volume, *Die Traumdeutung* (*The Interpretation of Dreams*), which appeared in 1900, was a trumpet call announcing the thought trends of the new century.

Time as Knowledge

The part played by the unconscious in subsequent literature will be noted as various individual works are discussed; some have been referred to already. Likewise, another of the century's leading ideas has been mentioned along with several imaginative works which make use of it: time. In a way that it formerly wasn't, time is now related to space. Einstein posited that time was another dimension of space, and much of the contemporary interest in space, outer and otherwise, is an extension of some of Einstein's theories about time.

Earlier, Jules Verne and H. G. Wells had pitched the imagination of man into outer space, in books that were entertaining melodramas; now, with space travel a reality, its literary expression remains in the realm of science-fiction stories, mostly claptrap, but in the future there is no doubt that space travel will become one of the subjects of serious literature since it will be an important part of man's experience. But this needn't bother us at the moment, for it will take such literature a long while to shake off its origins and emerge in its own right. Just now our concern is with the influence of time on twentieth-century books, in which time becomes a way of knowing.

Again, as with the investigations of the unconsciousness, this matter will be discussed in relation to individual works as we come to them. But a few more remarks of a general nature may be made in regard to time in contemporary literature. As previously pointed out, Lewis Mumford has traced the development of our time-regulated lives to the sounding of the monastery bells at set intervals. Merchants could arrange to meet and discuss business at a definite hour—say as the eighth bell pealed across the countryside and was heard in the closest town ("I will meet you at the corner of Assassination Street and Cutpurse Lane"). Nevertheless, for a long while, even with the multiplication of clocks, this use of the marking of intervals of time must have remained fairly casual. But at last the inventions of the nineteenth century brought about widespread scheduling and the ideas of speed which became so important to the man of the following century.

In the Middle Ages, the knight setting off from France on a crusade had no timetable to tell him precisely when he would arrive in Syria, and he had even less of an idea as to when he might be getting back home. Similarly, in the days of sailing ships, a man traveling from the eastern coast of the United States to China, by way of Cape Horn, had to think of his voyage there and back in terms of many months, sometimes of years. But finally the imperatives of scheduling took over. In the eighteenth century, the spread of stagecoach travel contributed toward the establishment of timetables. And, as Lewis Mumford has further pointed out, the factories of the Industrial Revolution, with their accurately measured working hours, also helped give time a dominance over men's lives. In the nineteenth century the railroad could estimate its travel time far more accurately than the old stagecoaches and, by the end of that period, the automobile had been invented, and the first airplane flights were soon to be made. In relation to cars, time regulation is important both as a potential of what various types attain to and as a legal factor in highway travel. Airplanes have speed limitations after takeoff which are ideally thought of as limited only by human endurance, and this can be increased artificially; even rockets have become an instrument of human travel.

The concept of time, then, is obviously and closely related to the speed at which people of this century move. True, many of them use speed for its own sake, and in numerous instances a man who moves very swiftly has no greater necessity to reach his destination earlier than the crusader making his way toward Acre or the sailor bound for China on a clipper ship—indeed, so many modern lives are so essentially bound up in trivial events that the man of today often has less reason for his speed. And many rapid travelers, such as the hot-rod gangs, make use of speed merely for exhilaration. There are, as always, compensatory factors; because of the increased speed of travel, accident victims can be rushed to hospitals more quickly, and people with genuine emergencies can arrive at their destinations earlier than would have been possible in the past. All these points are fairly obvious, but we should keep them in mind when reading any novel, story, play, or poem of today. Of course painting, music, sculpture and—most organically— vehicle design are also affected.

An Excursion into Art

Consider a few examples from art. Constantin Brancusi's sculpture of 1919, *Bird in Flight*, is a slender, upright, curved figure of bronze—it is impossible to describe, but one might say that the viewer on first seeing it has something of the impression of an airplane-propeller blade, though the outlines of the sculpture, however clean, are less formalized. In any event, the figure does at once give a suggestion of a rapid and high movement of flight. Now it is true that artists have in the past been concerned with motion, and that many paintings of birds going through the sky have caught the spirit of flight. But the point is that Brancusi had done this in a way that almost suggests technics; and his avoidance of the type of representation known as realism is modern indeed, for *Bird in Flight* (as well as the later—1924—Brancusi sculpture which closely resembles it, *Bird in Space*) is, without being abstract, a creation of pure form.

Consider a quite different portrayal of motion, one which, like Brancusi's could have been made only after the nineteenth century: Marcel Duchamp's *Nude Descending a Staircase.* Two versions of this may be found in the Philadelphia Museum, one painted in 1911 and the other (which was the sensation of the Armory Show in New York in 1913) painted in 1912. The first is more compact, with a somewhat more realistic suggestion of the staircase itself. The later version is motion fragmented, as if it were several strips from a moving-picture film (at that time an exciting new art-form). Considered philosophically, Duchamp's painting could be called a commentary on the space-time theories of the ancient philosopher Zeno of Elea who, considering the flight of an arrow and Achilles' mythical race with a tortoise, declared that "motion does not exist because the moving body must go half the distance before it goes the whole distance." Duchamp, of course, may not have been thinking of this argument, but his painting almost seems to be a reflection of it. Again, however, it must be stated that this could be only a twentieth-century reflection, distinctly so, representing the school of cubism, which more than any other in this age (except some phases of surrealism) dealt with space-time problems.

Another famous modern painting will provide a further idea as to how modern artists treat the time factor: Pablo Picasso's *Guernica*, in the Museum of Modern Art, New York. In scope, this painting may for all its difference in subject matter be compared to one of the sixteenth-century carnival paintings by Pieter Brueghel, in which a group of hearty Flemish men and women are flinging themselves wildly across the broad canvas. Or consider Brueghel's *Landscape with the Fall of Icarus*, of which W. H. Auden has written in his poem, "Musée des Beaux Artes" —

> *About suffering they were never wrong,*
> *The Old Masters: how well they understood*
> *Its human position; how it takes place*
> *While someone else is eating or opening a window or*
> > *just walking along.*

Auden applies this idea to the Brueghel painting which shows a plowman, a shepherd with his flock, a distant city, and some ships, one of which is close to the fallen sky-flier, whose leg alone remains out of the water; but

> *the expensive delicate ship that must have seen*
> *Something amazing, a boy falling out of the sky,*
> *Had somewhere to get to and sailed calmly on.*

Auden is making a special point here, which is connected with the simultaneity of events across the wide picture.

There are also the earlier paintings by Hieronymus Bosch, who likewise projected a vast simultaneous activity across great space: depicting sin or hell, Bosch would show a widely scattered group of people being penetrated by sword or clyster, crucified on harp or drowned in slime, activities carried out under the supervision of weird creatures combining the characteristics of various animals. All these events occur at the same instant across a wide space, so

that a single painting has the effect of being many pictures. There is, admittedly, a sense of the wholeness of the
experience which the viewer catches at first sight, and yet
in order to understand, really to *see* the painting, he must
take it up part by part, an exercise which emphasizes the
element of time and its relation to space. The surrealist
tendency is here, already, and will be noted later; just now,
consider the breadth, scope, and simultaneousness of the
action in a Bosch painting. These features are intensified in
Picasso, not only in *Guernica* but in various other pictures
as well, which use the technique of simultaneism.

There is Picasso's *The Death of Marat*, for example,
which is little known—at least it is seldom reproduced.
Compare this with Jacques Louis David's *Marat Dead* in
his Bathtub, of which Crane Brinton says (in A *Decade of
Revolution: 1789–1799*), "Now merely an interesting
piece of realism, this [painting] was to the true Jacobin a
Pietà." David shows Marat just after the murder—he was a
man whom a skin disease kept in his bathtub a good part
of the time—leaning partway out of the tub, one hand
still holding a quill pen, the other grasping the sheet on
which he had been writing. A long, spadelike knife lies on
the floor, blood streaks down from a wound in the subject's
chest, and the turbaned Marat looks very dead: every line of
his body contributes to this effect. It is, as Professor Brinton says, an interesting example of realism, and it shows
rather precisely all the details which the retina of anyone
present would pick out. But Picasso's painting is altogether
different, and when juxtaposed with David's it demonstrates how far we have come; it reveals what is truly modern.

Picasso shows the moment of assassination, with wild
action conveyed by flying lines. As in David's painting, the
blood and the knife are there, but not statically: the knife
is being forced downward, and the blood is gushing from
the wound. Marat seems dead at once; the figure that
catches the eye is at the left, a dishevelled Charlotte
Corday, a figure which in design makes no pretense of the
everyday realism of the retina but, because of the intensity
with which the artist has worked, she seems more real than

"real": she is the very incarnation of terror and terrorism. Her mouth is not merely wide open, it is distended beyond probability in some kind of frantic scream, her hair is flying (a few short lines), and her eye is either repeated (or is it both eyes?) in improbable parts of her face, intensifying the effect of fright and frightfulness; and there is still another eye, across the room in a kind of window whose entering light repeats the triangular shape of the dagger, reflected in other triangular motifs in the picture—which is altogether a picture of ferocious effectiveness.

It is certainly a forerunner of *Guernica*, originally painted for the Paris Exhibition of 1937—for the building there representing the legally elected government of Spain. The painting is among other things an example of propaganda, a very powerful example of it: the subject is the world's first massive air raid, when General Franco employed the Nazi planes at his disposal to smash the Basque town of Guernica. Picasso, who is part Basque, used again some of the techniques of *The Death of Marat*, particularly the distorted mouths and confused eyes, to convey the horror of the air raid which killed a thousand civilians. The electric light in an eyelike setting, the ritualistic bull, the tormented faces and flung-out arms, the screaming horse—all these elements, in a masterful composition of violent lines and jagged planes, combine to make the huge mural canvas the modern world's most compelling artistic testimony, so far, to the frightfulness of modern warfare. Once again, the painting is emphatically a twentieth-century creation, not merely in its subject matter but even more so in its technique.

Guernica is in the vein of surrealism, with some elements of cubism in it. As John Goulding says in *Cubism: A History and an Analysis, 1907–1914*, "*Guernica* is not a cubist painting, but equally obviously it could not have come into being without cubism behind it." The influence of this movement appears not only in the geometrization of planes and angles found in so much modern art, but also in such offshoots of cubism as simultaneism. Sir Herbert Read defined the latter as the combining of "different aspects of figures and objects in the same painting"—as in those oddly placed and fiercely staring eyes in the *Marat* and *Guernica* figures.

Something very much like simultaneism is, as will be shown now, paralleled in some of the important literature of our epoch. To mention some significant examples, consider Gertrude Stein (whose work is often simultaneist) or the "Wandering Rocks" section of James Joyce's *Ulysses*, a part of the book which describes many things occurring in different parts of Dublin at the same time. There is, for instance, the sentence, "Corny Kelleher sped a silent jet of hayjuice arching from his mouth while a generous white arm from a window in Eccles Street flung forth a coin." This needs a little explanation. A begging one-legged sailor has been described earlier as near Mountjoy Square, which is not too far from Eccles Street, toward which he is lurching, and which he arrives at by the time Molly Bloom is shown flinging out the coin. But in the first part of the sentence describing Molly's action, we have Corny Kelleher spitting; and he has been previously located chewing on a blade of hay while totting up figures in H. J. O'Neills' funeral establishment. This is at Newcome Bridge, many streets away from Eccles. Joyce tells more of Corny Kelleher, and elsewhere even finishes the description of Molly's flinging the coin (it went "over the area railings. It fell on the path")—but in that sentence quoted earlier, Joyce has provided (as he does throughout the "Wandering Rocks" and in other parts of *Ulysses*) a perfect example of the adaptation of simultaneism to literature. Note how the quotation applies to what has been said about the use of time theories by moderns, and how it also fits in with what has been said of paintings from Brueghel's to Picasso's.

Consider, too, Virginia Woolf's description in *Mrs. Dalloway*, of the feelings of the neurotic ex-soldier, Septimus Smith: "He lay very high, on the back of the world. The earth thrilled beneath him. Red flowers grew through his flesh; their stiff leaves rustled by his head. Music began clanging against the rocks up here. . . . It cannoned from rock to rock, divided, met in shocks of sound which rose in smooth columns (that music should be visible was a discovery) and became an anthem, an anthem twined round now by a shepherd piping." Commenting on this passage, Lewis Mumford in his essay, "Surrealism and Civilization," asks: "Need I point out that one has only to transfer these images onto canvas to have a complete surrealist painting?"

Comparisons of literature and art are as old as criticism itself. Plato said the poet was like a painter, and Aristotle, in discussing poetry, several times remarked, "It is the same in painting." But Horace put the relationship into a slogan that became famous: *ut pictura poesis* (as in a painting, so in a poem). Such concepts have their perils, and Gotthold Ephraim Lessing pointed some of them out in the eighteenth century, in his *Laokoön*; but, as Jean Hagstrom has shown in *The Sister Arts* (1958), Lessing was primarily attacking the tendencies, in his time, of writers who overpictorialized: "The more one considers the essential elements of Lessing's treatise, the more one becomes convinced that his critical guns were trained at very minor writers indeed—perhaps the lesser German descriptive poets of the early eighteenth century—and not at the richly allusive, highly compressed, visually sharp, but emotionally evocative pictorialism of neoclassic poetic art at its best." The main theme of Professor Hagstrom's book is that writers are often sensitive to the effects of painting, and adopt them. And certainly in our time there is a close relationship between painting and literary expression: the work of various writers suggests, in different ways, pictures by an Oskar Kokoschka, a Maurice Utrillo, a Jackson Pollack, an Edvard Munch, sometimes in creating intensity by distortion of form, sometimes by using words that have the effect of tonality or the quality of pigments.

The New Sound of Music

What of the relationship between literature and music in the twentieth century? E. M. Forster, one of the finest novelists practicing in English in this era, said that "fiction is likely to find its nearest parallel" in music.

Yet much, if not most, music is abstract: a sonata or even a symphony can exist entirely in its own terms, needing no more identification than a catalogue number. Nevertheless, there is a good deal of programmatic music that tries to be somewhat literary, though unless the composer has provided a helpful title or notes, the listener may not be altogether sure of what he is hearing: the piece may be intended to represent a battle—or just a storm.

In some ways, music was ahead of twentieth-century fiction in making use of modernistic effects. Richard Wagner's employment of the leitmotif, for example, foreshadows the stream-of-consciousness novel. Interestingly enough, Wagner didn't use the term leitmotif, now so frequently credited to him; but the principle is in his music, for when Tristan thinks of Isolde, the Isolde theme enters his song; when Siegfried remembers Brunhilde, the chords defining her take over the music. Now Wagner was an immensely influential force, in literature the idol of the French symbolist school. But Wagner and his immediate followers, such as Gustav Mahler, Anton Bruckner, and Richard Strauss, left music exhausted. Claude Debussy, Erik Satie, and Igor Stravinsky were liberating influences who, in the 1890s and in the early twentieth century, opened the way for such evolutions in music as atonality.

Debussy, who had affinities both with the impressionist painters and the symbolist poets, manifested literary interest when he wrote his *Prélude à l'après-midi d'un faune*, (*Prelude to the Afternoon of a Faun*), suggesting a poem by Stéphane Mallarmé, official leader of the symbolists. The music itself was revolutionary, however, as was Debussy's opera, taken from Maurice Maeterlinck's symbolical play, *Pelléas et Mélisande* (1902). But the revolution here was quiet enough, though not without protest; the riots came later, in 1913, at the première, in Paris, of Stravinsky's *Le Sacre du printemps* (*The Rite of Spring*), performed by the Diaghilev ballet—as much of it as could be performed under handicaps.

One of these handicaps was the audience, whose shouts

of rage drowned out the music. To the dancers, however (Pierre Monteux was the conductor, Vaslav Nijinsky the choreographer), the music itself was a handicap; according to Diaghilev's régisseur at the time, S. L. Grigoriev, the company had heartily disliked the rehearsals, "calling them arithmetic classes, because owing to the total absence of tune in the music, the dancers had to time their movements by counting the bars."

But if the performers in their disapproval were a little ahead of the public, they, like the public, were in turn eventually drowned out, for *Sacre* has become one of the standard ballets. *Sacre*, incidentally, reflects an important art trend of the early twentieth century: primitivism. After 1905, Henri Matisse and a group of painters associated with him became known as *les Fauves* (the wild beasts) because their work projected a violent simplicity. In Germany, the painters of *die Brücke* (the bridge) group were inspired by Ernst Ludwig Kirchner, who himself had been inspired by African sculptures in the Berlin Museum. There were of course independent primitives, too, such as Paul Gauguin and Henri Rousseau. In music, *Le Sacre du printemps* was one of the first attempts to make the primitive melodic—or, rather, unmelodic.

Debussy, in the opera *Pelléas*, had abandoned the aria for a monotone close to human speech. One critic, Léon Kerst, said the morning after the first performance, "All I heard—for even when you don't understand a thing you can't go to the theater without hearing something—well, all I heard was a series of harmonized sounds—I don't say harmonious—which succeeded one another, uninterruptedly, without a single phrase, a single motif, a single accent, a single form, a single outline. And to this accompaniment, unnecessary singers drone out words, nothing but words, a kind of long-drawn-out monotonous recitative, unbearable, moribund!" Debussy, it is plain, had offended, though not to the extent that Stravinsky and his followers did eleven years later. But then the atonalists came along, and music was indeed modern, if somewhat incomprehensibly so.

Arnold Schönberg, born in Vienna, was in his youth

greatly influenced by his friend and master, Mahler, but by 1907, when Schönberg's *First String Quartet* had its première, it was sufficiently "advanced" to cause the audience to hiss and stamp. Yet this was some years before Schönberg hit upon atonality, which he preferred to call pantonality. Thomas Mann used Schönberg's musical style for part of that of his composer in *Doctor Faustus*, and this greatly enraged Schönberg. Here is one excellent example of the closeness of literature and music, for Schönberg forced Mann's publishers, in later editions of the book, to insert a postscript explaining the composer's property rights to the musical techniques described in the story. But, for Adrian Leverkühn, Mann had also drawn upon Mahler, Hugo Wolf, and other composers, as well as upon the philosopher Nietzsche. The acknowledgment to Schönberg was included in the book against his own conviction, Mann said, "not so much because such an explanation knocks a small breach into the rounded, integral world of my novel, as because, within the sphere of the book, within this world of a pact with the devil and of black magic, the idea of the twelve-tone technique assumes a coloration and a character which it does not possess in its own right and which—is this not so?—in a sense makes it really my property, or, rather, the property of the book." Mann felt his ad hoc version and Schönberg's idea were so greatly different that it would have been insulting to have mentioned Schönberg in the text.

The twelve-tone technique Mann referred to is one that lacks the traditional harmonic features; if Debussy had to some extent led toward this, he had done so harmoniously; Schönberg achieved his own effects contrapuntally. His system—followed by Alban Berg and Anton von Webern, among others—abandoned the old concepts of consonance and dissonance; its effect tends to be vertical rather than horizontal (time-span). The atonal composers use recurring themes; indeed, the traditional method of relating musical impulses to the auditory sense has not changed in this music, but the momentary relationship—the vertical sounds—have no logical or functional relationship to each other.

Because of this, the individual moments may sound chaotic, unrelated, angular, and dissonant, but these moments occur repeatedly in the total structure, and the more the ear can retain of these entities, the clearer the music is; but most listeners find it difficult to organize these chaotic impressions into unities. For the twelve-tone system, instead of having a keynote dominating all other sounds, has twelve distinct sounds, each within a semitone of the next. This kind of tonal anarchy is what many of the twentieth-century prose writers indulge in, or did in the more experimental phases of the era. Gertrude Stein, for example, in *The Making of Americans* (written 1906–8 but not published until 1925), was using language somewhat atonally when she wrote

> Every one then is an individual being. Every one then is like many others always living, there are many ways of thinking of every one, this is now a description of all of them. There must then be a whole history of each one of them. There must then now be a description of all repeating. Now I will tell all the meaning to me in repeating, the loving there is in me for repeating.

This is a fairly simple and comprehensible passage from *The Making of Americans*, which is a novel that runs to a thousand pages, most of whose paragraphs have just such comma splices and just such violations of "normal" grammar as the one quoted. Granted, prose usually has conceptual suggestions different from those of music, and these are present in Gertrude Stein's prose, as they are present in the singing lines of Joyce's *Finnegans Wake* and in the jumbled tones of the stream of consciousness as represented in parts of Faulkner's *The Sound and the Fury*; but the resemblance to atonality is there.

Sometimes when writing is compared to music, one considers form rather than sound, as in E. M. Forster's enquiry as to whether there is "any effect in novels comparable to the effect of the *Fifth Symphony* [Beethoven's] as a whole, where when the orchestra stops, we hear something that has never actually been played? The opening movement, the andante, and the trio-scherzo-trio-finale-trio-finale that composes the third block, all enter the mind at once, and extend one another into a common entity," which is of course the symphony as a whole. Forster couldn't find any analogy when he wrote this passage for the Clark lectures at Cambridge, published in 1927 as *Aspects of the Novel*, but he admitted that one might exist; and certainly if there is none in the novel, at least T. S. Eliot admittedly followed a musical pattern in *Four Quartets*, completed in 1943; they have a musiclike form, and they admittedly suggest Beethoven.

Poetry is, of course, nearer to the sound effects of music than fictional writing often is; yet Joyce, Stein, and others have definite points of correspondence with modern composers, often at thematic as well as at other levels. In writing of Aaron Copland in *Music and Society* (1950), Wilfrid Mellers might almost be speaking of John Dos Passos when he says that "Copland's music is imbued with a feeling, peculiar to big industrial cities, both of man's antlike energy and his ineluctable loneliness. The suggestion of timelessness in his work is thus not unconnected with America's physical, geographical vastness."

In literature, in the visual arts, and in music, there are kinships of modernity which mark the art products of this century as distinctive to their time. The foregoing contains only a few suggestions of what these kinships are, which derive from yesterday and the day before yesterday and from the deepest thinking and feeling out of man's past, wrought into the attitudes and art forms of the present epoch. It might be said, at the very least, that the matters mentioned in the foregoing are somewhere in the consciousness of every modern creator of literature whose work is worth reading.

22

Thomas Wolfe

Looking Homeward Again?

"The mountains were my masters," Thomas Wolfe noted in 1924, "the unyielding mountains which were beyond the necessity of growth and change." He put that down in a hitherto unpublished travel diary on his first trip to Europe at the age of twenty-four, when publication of his first novel, *Look Homeward, Angel,* lay just five years ahead. That sentence in his journal was prophetic of all his writings, for although he struggled to achieve growth and change before his death at thirty-seven, his talent remained unyielding, and his fiction had the fixed and jagged immensity of a mountain range.

Critics have tended to deal severely with Wolfe because his novels are almost invariably and exhaustingly autobiographical, and because he too often yielded to the enticements of a Southern-style rhetoric that became repetitious, bloated, and wearying. Yet he was always an intense observer who could vigorously record grotesqueries of human behavior, so that even if his central figure remained rather monotonously the same ("O lost!"), he was often surrounded by vital characters who, though also not growing, stood out as vivid and engaging, often attractively comic.

The story of Wolfe and the two publishers' editors—Maxwell Perkins and Edward C. Aswell—who struggled to give some unity to his work is sufficiently well known to need no

The Notebooks of Thomas Wolfe. Edited by Richard S. Kennedy and Paschal Reeves. University of North Carolina Press. (*Saturday Review,* March 7, 1970. Copyright 1970 by Saturday Review, Inc. Reprinted by permission.)

retelling here, but it must be said that the *Notebooks* now add greatly to our understanding of the ordeal of those two men and of Wolfe's own ambitions and purposes. As for the editors of these volumes of his journals, they too were under drastic pressure as they worked for five strenuous years in deciphering Wolfe's often smudged penciled scrawls. But these editors deserve congratulations, not only for their magnifying-glass labors, but also for the way in which, by digging through thirty-three pocket notebooks, one ledger, and a great many loose papers, they have carried out their intention to "present a kind of interior biography of Wolfe beginning with his years at Harvard, the time of his first serious literary endeavors."

At the end of their two volumes the editors include the last of Wolfe's writings—except for some letters—"A Western Journal," parts of which have been published before. About one-tenth of the available material in these notebooks is left out, including repetitious statistics concerning cities, people, and books, as well as grocery lists, American Express Travelers' Cheque numbers, and similar matters. One necessary and beguiling omission is noted in a deadpan way among some items of 1934: "At this point Wolfe sets down a list of the women with whom he has had sexual relations in the United States and the states in which they were born." For the sake of the curious it might be added that most of this material, including the revelations mentioned here, is at Harvard, though perhaps scrupulously guarded.

Despite such exclusions, a good many lists do occur in the text—authors of various countries, projected characters, recording of royalties—but, perhaps surprisingly, these are often interesting. The most absorbing passages, however, are Wolfe's instant registry of places or people, hasty and often unpunctuated jottings. They represent his gift for observation, and they come up from the page bright and living, as they might not when incorporated into his grandiloquent sentences. Such rough notations often inform the "internal autobiography" and also provide some piquant travelogue passages, European and American. There are also numerous fairly long "written-out" sections which supply

examples of Wolfe's early drafts of published and occasionally unpublished novels, stories, or sketches.

In assembling all this material, the editors have usually
been expert and accurate, yet with so much to manipulate
they were bound to make some slips which can easily be
corrected in a possible second printing. They say, for example, that they have inserted the French and German accent
marks which Wolfe so frequently omitted, *accent aigu* or
Umlaut, yet a number of names occur without the necessary marks, among them Cézanne, Avenue Kléber, Walküre,
and Molière, to name a few. The Spanish painter Zurbarán
becomes Zurberan, and the French playwright Simon Gan-
tillon appears as Goutillon, a somewhat pardonable error of
transcription. One of the editors' notes says that when
Wolfe saw "the Aldingtons" in Paris in 1930, Richard
Aldington's "wife, Hilda Doolittle, the Imagist poet, was
with him"; it is true that until 1937 Aldington was still married to the poet known as H. D., but the "Mrs. Aldington"
of that Paris occasion was Brigit Patmore. Also, the editors
state in a note that Robert McAlmon was the original of
Bill Gorton in Hemingway's *The Sun Also Rises;* but Gorton was taken from Donald Ogden Stewart. Sometimes,
however, the editorial notes inadvertently correct previous
misstatements made by other writers, as when they quote
a Wolfe letter mentioning a dinner party, thereby showing
that the original of the poet Rosalind Bailey in Wolfe's third
novel, *The Web and the Rock,* was not Edna St. Vincent
Millay, as the late Richard Chase said (calling her Rosa-
mund Bailey, in his 1960 introduction to that book), but
rather Elinor Wylie, a fact which Chase could have picked
up in the 1956 edition of the *Letters.*

Most of these issues are minor. The important point is
that the editing of these *Notebooks* is sound in the major
considerations. One of the editors, Richard S. Kennedy, in
1962 brought out *The Window of Memory,* a valuable
forerunner of these new volumes. And last year a book by
the other editor, Paschal Reeves, *Thomas Wolfe's Alba-
tross: Race and Nationality in America,* also led the way to
these *Notebooks,* in which Wolfe's xenophobia frequently

manifests itself. As the editors comment, because Wolfe
never properly accepted the diversity of origins and beliefs
among Americans he could not, in this area of the national
experience, "qualify as the epic spokesman because he
lacked the wide embrace of a Whitman." To him, blacks
were usually niggers, he wrote unfriendily of Americanized
"foreign types," and he was, as these *Notebooks* consistently
show, far more anti-Semitic than his apologists seem to have
known. He was, it is plain, genuinely in love with Mrs.
Aline Bernstein, his mistress across several years, but in his
journals he usually referred to her, with an evident but perhaps partly unconscious resentment, as "my Jew" or "the
Jew." These volumes contain the draft of a 1934 letter to
her that was cruelly anti-Semitic; apparently Wolfe had
the good grace not to copy it out and send it. The editors
point out that Wolfe is usually assumed to have developed
his anti-Semitism after a long series of quarrels with Mrs.
Bernstein, but they include an early diary-fragment from his
Harvard years which shows how deeply the anti-Jewish
clichés were embedded in his consciousness.

Yet Wolfe escaped at least partly from such attitudes
toward the end of his life, as his long story, "I Have a Thing
to Tell You," demonstrates. It also reveals his post-1936
disillusionment with Germany, previously his favorite foreign
country. As readers of that novella know, it was the Nazis'
vicious treatment of a Jew trying to get out of Germany
which turned Wolfe against the régime. When he began to
write the story in Paris, as soon as he arrived there in September 1936, he started the third paragraph, "I don't like
Jews"—but he cut that qualification later, for he had a thing
to tell us.

You Can't Go Home Again was the title his editor gave
to Wolfe's last novel, after the author's death; the phrase
was one he had often used. Yet in the last two years of
his life he *was* in some ways going home again, and in
those years he not only explored a large part of Western
America but made his first visit in eight years to his native
Asheville, the Altamont and Lybia Hill of his novels. If he
had lived he might have discovered for himself a new America. Certainly he was jaded, at least in those last years, with

Europe. After leaving Germany in 1936 he stopped at Paris en route to New York, and the French capital he had always rejoiced in—particularly its restaurants and cafés—he described on that last autumn visit as a "sad and enervating town." He complained of "The eternal monotony of French life—The banal life of cafés—the people gesticulating and talking—and to what purpose?" This was quite different from his lively impressions of the past, as in the spring of 1935—

> The queer smoky bright light of Paris in morning . . . old man with whiskers bearing bottle—another old man caped and capped (pocket with leather bag beneath)—boy pumps by on tricycle piled with great wicker baskets . . . workers going by—little solid Frenchman bandy legged—cap—white scarf—heavy suit—*worker*—where—Some well dressed men—workers also—others (workers) in denim earnestly pedaling bikes—stump cigar holding in mouth.

There is no such animation in the 1936 notes (quoted earlier); Wolfe merely mentions the places at which he ate and drank, obviously with little zest, and he adds some censure of the American expatriates who had celebrated Paris in the 1920s, and who in his view had produced nothing worthwhile.

Like many of his fellow writers of the time, however, Wolfe soon veered somewhat to the left, writing for liberal journals and even, in the case of a story he could have sold for a profit, presenting the piece gratis to the *New Masses*. Like so many liberal or United Front writers of the day, he began speaking of people whom he didn't like as Fascists, and in a 1937 entry in these *Notebooks* he amusingly listed "Potential Fascist Literary Groups and Individuals," and lo! the *Saturday Review*'s name led all the rest. Wolfe had been furious at the *Saturday Review*'s editor, Bernard DeVoto, for his 1936 review ("Genius is not Enough") of Wolfe's *The Story of a Novel*, which had first appeared as a three-part serial in the *Saturday Review* in 1935, the year in which Wolfe's second novel, *Of Time and the River*, came out. That book had, with certain qualifications, been treated favorably by the departing editor of the *Saturday Review* (one of its founders, Henry Seidel Canby, who retired that year into a contributing editorship). Wolfe's agent, Elizabeth Nowell, in her 1960 biography of her author, recalled that Canby's was "the first major review to turn the tide in favor of *Of Time and the River*." But Wolfe had something of a tendency toward megalomania, which went with his mountainous image of himself, and you had to be with him one hundred percent of the way or you were altogether against him. And although DeVoto's name occurred in the potential-Fascist enumeration, Canby's didn't; but Wolfe's inevitable denigration of Canby appeared in the last posthumous collection of his fiction, *The Hills Beyond* (1941), which depicted the *Saturday Review* founder in that rather crude pasquinade, "Portrait of a Literary Critic," dated by Aswell as "after 1935." It is interesting to note that Wolfe further included in his "Fascist" list not only the *New York Times Book Review*, but also its editor at that time, J. Donald Adams. The *Virginia Quarterly Review* qualified too, as did the Southern Agrarians and the literary newspaper columns of Herschel Brickell and Harry Hansen. The *New York Sun* was likewise blasted, along with the American Academy of Arts and Letters, to say nothing of the National Institute (Wolfe called it the Academy) of Arts and Letters, in which Wolfe had not long before accepted membership. But after the appearance of his first book, he sometimes felt hostility toward other writers or was at least uncomfortable with them, and he didn't get along particularly well even with F. Scott Fitzgerald and Ernest Hemingway, though Perkins wanted all Scribner's authors to be happy together.

Yet there are signs that Wolfe was mellowing toward the end of his life. Before he left Paris for that last time in 1936, he wrote, in the fragmentary first draft of "I Have a Thing to Tell You," some words that he of course meant for all mankind: ". . . brothers, we must brothers be—or die," a curious anticipation of the famous line in the early versions of W. H. Auden's "September 1, 1939": "We must love one another or die." Perhaps after all, Thomas Wolfe was, in a most human way, really preparing to go home again.

23

Zelda

Zelda Sayre married F. Scott Fitzgerald in April 1920 and became the Golden Girl of his novels and stories, as well as the heroine of the couple's flagrant escapades in New York and Hollywood and on the Riviera. Zelda whirled through the decade which Fitzgerald christened the Jazz Age and, in April 1930, exactly ten years after her marriage, she suffered her first mental breakdown. Through the years of Depression and war she was continually in and out of sanatoriums until her death in 1948.

The general story of Zelda Fitzgerald has been told in the biographies dealing with her husband: Arthur Mizener's brilliant, scholarly volume and Andrew Turnbull's popular-style production. But in both these books Zelda appears only in direct relation to events concerning her husband. Henry Dan Piper's *F. Scott Fitzgerald: A Critical Portrait*, although not primarily biographical, devotes a chapter to Zelda's novel, *Save Me the Waltz*, and tells more about her ancestral background than other writers had. But until Nancy Milford's book, no one has presented the full-length portrait of Zelda Fitzgerald which she eminently deserves, as the present volume consistently shows.

It began as a master's thesis at Columbia University, and Mrs. Milford spent seven years on it. The result is what might be called an example of the New Biography, which at

Zelda. By Nancy Milford. Harper and Row. (*New York Times Book Review*, June 14, 1970. © 1970 by The New York Times Company. Reprinted by permission.)

its best can be painstakingly thorough without smothering the subject under the weight of the documentation. About a quarter-century ago, some extremists among critics who tried to demonstrate that literary texts existed in a vacuum, and that the lives and milieux of authors had no bearing on their work, nearly stamped out literary biographies. They managed to survive, however, often more exhaustively detailed in recent years than their predecessors had been. An outstanding example of the New Biography, Richard Ellmann's *James Joyce*, scrupulously examines every ingredient, major or minor, of Joyce's experience, and yet the Irish author steps through the book's pages as a living figure, as Zelda Fitzgerald does in Mrs. Milford's biography.

In preparing it she interviewed not only those who had previously written about Fitzgerald, but also friends of the couple who had already talked or corresponded with these authors. Like Louis Sheaffer, who doubled back on familiar trails for the first of his so-far-published volumes on Eugene O'Neill, Mrs. Milford often extracted new material from old sources. But she also saw and exchanged letters with a good many people who hadn't been approached earlier, not only youthful friends of Zelda, but also doctors who had attended her, both in European hospitals and at the Phipps Clinic (Johns Hopkins) in Baltimore, as well as the one in Asheville, North Carolina.

The branch of psychology which deals with aberrations had its true literary beginnings toward the end of the nineteenth century, when Sigmund Freud and Richard von Krafft-Ebing undertook the publication of case histories, of course using no names, of the piquant behavior of little Viennese shoeclerks, housemaids, or sausage salesmen. The present book, which takes the usual narrative-biography form, is in most respects not like those case histories, though parts of it have a clinical atmosphere and authority rarely found in biographies. This one of course has the range of a full-length life history, and a special importance because of its relation to modern American literature.

On the psychological side, readers will be particularly

interested to learn—and the author passes on the information rather unobtrusively—that Zelda's father once had a nine-months' breakdown, that one of her sisters was subject to nervous spells, and that her maternal grandmother was a suicide.

On both sides, the family was of distinguished Southern stock, and Mrs. Milford deals interestingly with the ancestral relationships. Zelda's imaginative mother, a thwarted actress, named her youngest child after a gypsy queen in a novel.

The little girl was sharply clever from the first, and vigorously independent. As she grew up, she retained the frolicsome ways of her childhood and often shocked the girls who knew her. One of her capers which Mrs. Milford writes of for the first time tells a good deal about her subject: as Zelda was passing a photographer's shop one night in Montgomery, some of her high-school acquaintances began taunting her because the lighted window displayed a picture of one of her beaus who was there in a fancy frame rather than actually with her, so Zelda kicked a hole in the glass and marched off with the picture.

It must be said at once that this was a far different kind of behavior from that practiced by Scott Fitzgerald in his boyhood and youth in St. Paul, at a minor Eastern prep school, and at Princeton. In those years he simply didn't indulge in Zelda's kind of pranks, for he poignantly wanted to "belong." He was never admired in those years so much as he had hoped to be, partly because he couldn't conform to what he could only regard, however unconsciously, as mediocre group-standards. But at Princeton he at least became a member of the Triangle and Cottage clubs and the good friend of Edmund Wilson and several other campus intellectuals.

Zelda in her youth went a lonelier way. She "did not have the knack," Mrs. Milford's researches have shown her, "for forming close friendships with girls her own age; she didn't belong to any of their clubs, and she was not invited to their overnight parties." This daughter of a conservative judge became, perhaps partly in defiance of his strictness, the kind of girl known as "fast"—so she was at least popular with the boys.

While she was still in high school, the First World War broke out, and infantrymen and flyers crowded into the training camps near Montgomery. Scott Fitzgerald was one of the younger officers who met Zelda at the local country club, and he began the hectic twenty-two-months' court-ship that ended in their marriage in New York. Fitzgerald's letters to Zelda in this interim have apparently not survived, but he carefully saved those she wrote to him. Mrs. Milford quotes from them extensively for the first time. They are not remarkable, but like most intimate love letters they drama-tize the writer and the situation, and in these communica-tions a phrase flashes out now and then to show that Zelda had a natural, however minor, gift for writing. Fitzgerald actually used parts of these letters, as well as of Zelda's diary, in fashioning the character of Rosalind in *This Side of Paradise*, published just a week before their marriage. It was his first novel, and the beginning of his first, short-lasting burst of fame.

There was also notoriety, for the conspicuously glamorous couple rode through Manhattan on the tops of taxis, dived into public fountains, and performed other antics which, it must be stressed, were probably instigated by Zelda rather than her husband. Here was youth, the newly emancipated youth which Fitzgerald typified in his stories, soon to be celebrated as representing the spirit of the rampaging twen-ties.

The Fitzgeralds, in the fashionable defiance of the time, drank heavily, although alcohol didn't become a problem to Zelda as it did to her husband, who at various levels was a pathetically vulnerable human being. As the pair grew somewhat older, their friends became increasingly weary of all the stunts, some of which suggested latent antagonisms —against each other or against life itself—which in the course of time would reach the surface. There was, for exam-ple, the occasion (reported by Gerald Murphy) when they were quarreling and Zelda lay down in front of their car, which failed to start, or her husband would have deliber-

ately run over her; and once Zelda, in a story related by
Sara Murphy, egged Fitzgerald into attempting dangerous
dives from high rocks above the sea at Antibes, herself
leading the way with her own desperate plunges.

These events apparently occurred in the middle 1920s, at
a time when Fitzgerald was helping Ernest Hemingway toward publication in America. Hemingway realized long before his friend did that Zelda was jealous of her husband's
work, with which she often interfered. In an agony of com-
petition she resumed the ballet lessons of her youth, at an
age when she was beyond achieving any important success
as a dancer, and the strain of her effort helped toward her
1930 breakdown. Enter the doctors.

And now the story intensifies. Fitzgerald in his most important novels, *The Great Gatsby* (1925) and *Tender is the
Night* (1934), as well as in *The Last Tycoon*, unfinished
but notably excellent, and in some of his finest stories,
showed that a grim darkness often lurked behind the golden
light of an age that worshipped glamour. This applies especially to *Tender is the Night*, in which midnight blackness
can abruptly close over Nicole's mind amid the glare of
Riviera sunlight. In his 1931 essay, "Echoes of the Jazz
Age," Fitzgerald said that, "by 1927 a wide-spread neurosis
began to be evident," and he added that various contemporaries of his "had begun to disappear into the dark maw
of violence."

Exactly how much Fitzgerald drew upon Zelda's clinical
ordeals for his portrait of Nicole in *Tender is the Night*
has never been so clearly shown as in some of the letters
of the early thirties, published here for the first time, between Zelda and her husband and, from both of them, to
the doctors involved. But this correspondence, most of the
documents lengthy and searching, is a good deal more than
part of the background material of a novel. It is important
biographically, not only because it helps to complete the
picture of Zelda, but also because it increases our knowledge of Scott Fitzgerald and his work.

This biography cannot seriously be called sensational,
though it makes some striking revelations. But these are

salient biographical points, and they will hardly embarrass living people. As an example, Fitzgerald told one of his wife's doctors, a woman at the Johns Hopkins hospital, that Zelda had been his mistress for a year before they were married, a previously unpublished bit of news which casts a significant light across the couple's tormented relationship (Fitzgerald was then so innocent, sexually, that he accepted Zelda's taunts about his genital proportions, as Hemingway reveals in the chapter called "A Matter of Measurements" in A *Moveable Feast*). In 1932, when Zelda was at a clinic in Baltimore, and Fitzgerald was trying to write in Montgomery, he ruefully wrote to her physician, Dr. Mildred Squires of Johns Hopkins, that "he was living in a state of 'mild masturbation and a couple of whiskeys to go on.'" That little note would probably not have appeared in a biography a dozen years ago. In this book, Fitzgerald's relationship with a Hollywood ingénue of the twenties is for the first time called an "affair" (his word). One of the real jolts here is a charge that Zelda first made perhaps a few years before her first breakdown, when she dramatically accused Fitzgerald of having a love affair with Hemingway.

Mrs. Milford doesn't pound all this information into one paragraph, but distributes it throughout the book, which for the most part focuses on those last nerve-tortured eighteen years of Zelda's life, about which so little has previously been known.

Early in her psychosis Zelda stayed at the elegant Swiss sanatorium, Les Rives de Prangins, which provides part of the setting for *Tender is the Night*. She was once examined by the famous Dr. Eugen Bleuler, inventor of the word *schizophrenia*, which he and other physicians readily applied to her, although one of them, Dr. Oscar Forel, recently told Mrs. Milford that he would now use a different term: "Apart from the clinical and classical forms . . . certain symptoms and behaviours or activities, are called *schizoid* and this does not mean that the person is schizophrenic." This particular bit of psychiatric scoring is not further explained by either Dr. Forel or Mrs. Milford.

Zelda's inner suffering at Prangins Sanatorium began to

show itself outwardly, and for months an eczema ate up the skin of her face, neck, and shoulders. One of those many letters from the patient to her husband which has not been published before projects her anguish and the pathos of her condition—

> *Please* help me. Every day more of me dies with this bitter and incessant beating I'm taking. . . . There's no justice— no quiet place of rest left in the world, and the longer I have to bear this the meaner and harder and sicker I get. . . . *Please* Please let me out now—Dear, you used to love me and I swear to you that this is no use. You must have seen. You said it was too good to spoil. What's spoiling is me, along with it and I don't see how any-body in the world has a right to do such a thing—

After fifteen months the Swiss doctors released Zelda, and for the last time she returned with her husband to America. He made two more trips to Hollywood, where he had been unsuccessful in a previous attempt to become a screen writer. On these later occasions, he traveled West alone, for in those years Zelda was going from one hospital to another, with intervals of freedom, usually at her mother's home in Montgomery. She dashed off some short stories which her husband's agent could sell, and she wrote her first novel, *Save Me the Waltz*. This book infuriated Fitzgerald because it unveiled so many intimacies of their marriage—his annoyance was ironical since the novel (*Tender*) which he was writing did exactly the same, and he was also annoyed because she was using his material. After some wrangling and a good deal of bowdlerizing, Zelda's volume was published in 1932. It was generally given low marks by the reviewers, who failed to note some of its interesting features that later readers have discovered.

Zelda began another novel a year or so after Fitzgerald had died in Hollywood in 1940, at the age of forty-four. Mrs. Milford synopsizes the unfinished *Caesar's Things* and quotes from it rather fully. The story is a confused one, giving somewhat different versions of people and incidents from those in the earlier novel, particularly in its treatment of Zelda's feelings, in 1924, toward the young French naval officer, Édouard Jozan, whom the Fitzgeralds knew on the Riviera.

Mrs. Milford, the only biographer on the Fitzgerald scene who has sought out Jozan, and the only one even to spell his name correctly, reports on his subsequent distinguished career as an admiral and suggests that he was perhaps not even aware "of Zelda's predicament." Mrs. Milford quotes Jozan to the effect that "Zelda's infidelity was imaginary. 'But they both had a need of drama, they made it up and perhaps they were the victims of their own unsettled and a little unhealthy imagination.'" Fitzgerald, however, said later that he "knew something had happened that could never be repaired." Once after the Jozan episode (or non-episode), Fitzgerald locked Zelda in, and once she nearly killed herself with an overdose of sleeping pills, as duly reported by the Murphys.

The clinical records which the industrious Mrs. Milford has consulted show that Zelda made feverish and paranoid complaints to the doctors ("in a highly idiosyncratic French" that Mrs. Milford translates) about her husband's supposed mistreatment of her after "a love affair with a French aviator in St. Raphael. I was locked in my villa for one month to prevent me from seeing him. This lasted for five years." When Zelda "knew" that Fitzgerald "had another woman in California," she told Dr. Forel in 1930, she said she was at first upset because she regarded life there as "so superficial, but finally I was not hurt because I knew I had done the same thing when I was younger." Interestingly enough, her novel *Caesar's Things* drifted away from her into a state of incompletion when she was unable to work out the problem of her heroine's attachment to "the flying officer who looked like a Greek God." Zelda herself had been, if not beautiful, at least attractively pretty, but her looks faded early, and her face became lined, grey-skinned, and hawklike.

Those who knew Zelda Fitzgerald in the last years of her life remember her vehement, evangelical religiosity. Mrs. Milford reports that Zelda sent pietistic letters, sometimes as mimeographed tracts, to her daughter and to old friends such as Edmund Wilson and Gertrude Stein. Once at a party at her home in Montgomery, Zelda fiercely told me, "God will destroy the United Nations because they used the atom bomb." She could be mildly amusing about her occasional instability and sometimes with a smile would excuse herself on the grounds that she was feeling "precarious." She was painting at this time, and one's memory of her intense pictures is mostly of their wildly disproportionate figures and, sometimes, an element of vibrant greenness.

Zelda's death in March 1948 was appalling. She was one of six women trapped in a fire on the top floor of that hospital in Asheville, North Carolina. "Her body was identified by a charred slipper lying beneath it." She was buried beside her husband in Rockville, Maryland, and so the story ends—but not really.

For, after Fitzgerald's death, his reputation flared up again. It has continued to burn steadily. And Zelda stands out as an important part of his personal and literary experience. Mrs. Milford's quotations of some 1947 remarks by Zelda about publication in a slick magazine's being "a goal worth seeking" may disturb some readers who know that Fitzgerald had to write a good many tawdry stories in order to live expensively, and that he felt that each effort of that kind drained away a part of his true talent.

Mrs. Milford points out that he contributed toward Zelda's breakdown, but it could hardly be said that he was the principal cause of it, any more than it can be asserted that Zelda "ruined" him, for every serious imaginative writer has tormenting problems to face, which only he can face at his lonely writing-table. "We ruined ourselves," Fitzgerald wrote to Zelda not long before he died. "I have never honestly thought that we ruined each other." Fitzgerald's own temperament was his most devitalizing handicap, one which he occasionally overcame; but those who admire his writings are grateful for his victories over it, and at this point there is no use in lamenting over the possibility that these victories could have been greater.

As for Zelda, she remains an archetype, concentrating the essential characteristics of the American girl of the time, not only as this girl appeared in the fiction of F. Scott Fitzgerald, but also in that of Cyril Hume, Katherine Brush, Stephen Vincent Benét, Dorothy Speare, "Warner Fabian," and others. Yet Zelda was also, and most perkily, an individual human being, one whose fundamentally artistic disposition helped to magnify her self-made difficulties. Mrs. Milford, writing a generally serviceable prose, presents Zelda in her various aspects in this scrupulously researched and never dull biography.

24

Style and Technique in the "Major Phase" of Henry James

"She waited [*comma*] Kate Croy [*comma*] for her father to come in . . ."

That is the opening clause of the first sentence in one of Henry James's last novels: *The Wings of the Dove:* "She waited, Kate Croy, for her father to come in . . ."—and the sentence goes on, to moderate length. But what an odd beginning for a work of fictional narrative. Any other writer would have said, "Kate Croy waited for her father to come in . . ." But Henry James is not any other writer.

We must, of course, consider the distinctiveness of his writing in relation to his meanings. In James, particularly in his later work, the meaning is usually complicated, intricately so, and to express it he needed a special kind of prose. He developed this in the last phase of his career as an author, a phase which began in the 1890s and ended with his death in 1916.

It is a phase which has often been parodied—notably by such admirers of Henry James as Max Beerbohm and James Thurber—parodied because of the prolixity of the sentences, with their elaborate phrasing and their excessive indirection. And yet, despite all witticisms and parodies at their expense, the three principal novels of that last period have survived, and many readers rewardingly find their way through them today.

Part of a lecture delivered at the University of California, Los Angeles, 1970.

These three novels are: *The Wings of the Dove* (1902), *The Ambassadors* (1903; actually written before the earlier-dated novel), and *The Golden Bowl* (1904). But before taking a close look at those novels, we might briefly consider some of the earlier writings of Henry James, as an introduction to the principal works of that last period, which the late F. O. Matthieson called "the major phase."

One of the principal concerns, throughout this essay, will be with the language of Henry James. Nowadays, many commentators on literature hesitate to use the word *style* in relation to an author's use of language. The term *style* has come to suggest a kind of adornment—not an organic element, but a frostinglike addition to the surface. As far back as 1936, T. S. Eliot, in writing an introduction to Djuna Barnes's novel, *Nightwood,* said that many readers might find the book somewhat strange because it was—and he was careful to use quotation marks—"written." A few years later Edmund Wilson, in explaining why he couldn't read Somerset Maugham, said—also using quotation marks—that Maugham's books were not "written." And, regrettably, most of the imaginative writing—fiction, that is—rolling off the presses these days is not "written." Too many writers of our time have merely turned out a grocery-list prose.

As for extended critical use of the word "written," it is probably too specialized in its meaning to be of much general use. So, if we don't like the word *style*, why not merely speak of an author's language, or his use of language?

As for the earlier writings of Henry James, they remain the favorites of many of his readers. But those who like the later work can also admire the earlier, and to speak of James's "major phase" is not to disparage what went before it, particularly such novels as *Daisy Miller,* say, of 1878 or *The Portrait of a Lady* of 1881.

James matured early as a writer, as an excellent and important writer, so that all his work beyond the very earliest beginnings may be read with admiration for its artistry. His themes are of profound interest to us today, particularly the one which critics called his "international theme," the confrontation of Americans with non-Americans. Various titles of some of his earlier novels and stories suggest this subject —*The American*, *The Europeans*, "An International Episode"—and even one of those last books, *The Ambassadors*, signals the theme. But this is only a part of James.

F. O. Matthieson could call an anthology of James's fiction *Stories of Writers and Artists*. A perceptive business-man turned critic, Osborn Andreas, wrote a book called *Henry James and the Expanding Horizon*, in which he shrewdly found, as a constant Jamesian pattern, "emotional cannibalism"—one human being feasting spiritually or emotionally off another. Andreas showed how this situation occurs throughout James's fiction.

Such themes inform the stories whose language we are now to consider.

James first really began to attain mastery about 1870, when he was twenty-seven years old and had been publishing stories for about six years. One feature of the better early works becomes clear at once: the language of the stories and novels of the 1870s and 1880s is not a language of the kind which, with appropriate quotation marks, can be called "dated." This qualification does not always apply to James's contemporaries or immediate predecessors, for example Nathaniel Hawthorne and Herman Melville. Hawthorne, with his vocabulary and cadences so often indebted to the past is, with all his somber intensity, often antiquated in sound and thought, and sometimes downright rhetorical. To say this is not to say, or in any sense imply, that in his major work he doesn't achieve some magnificent effects; but in the present consideration it is necessary to "place" him. Similarly, Melville often has an antique ring. Again, this is not said in disparagement, for in *Moby-Dick* for example, Melville's language frequently suggests the full power of the ocean and of the frenetic pursuit of that divine and demonic white whale—but, once more, we must judge the language with some exactitude, and when we do we often find Melville, here and elsewhere, committing hollow rhetoric. But—all homage to indomitable genius.

The language of Henry James is of a different kind. James in his early and middle years, when he is somewhat close in time to Hawthorne and Melville, does not sound antiquated; his language is essentially plain. Not that he is tame: there is force in his plainness. But in vocabulary, usage, and tone, the James of the 1870s and 1880s is distinctly modern, not in any way antiquated. The prose of his fiction of nearly a century ago could have been written this morning. (We should of course note that there was nothing of the antiquated in the work of several other contemporaries of James, such as Mark Twain, who were writing in a forceful, colloquial prose.)

Readers of James may, however, need a word of caution here, for some of his early work, as we have it today, represents revision. In the early 1900s he revised many of his novels and stories, and frequently in these reconstructions his later manner intruded upon the simpler prose of the past. His procedure sometimes brought about an improvement, in the subtilization and deepening of the material, though various textual editors of today prefer the earlier simplicity and believe that James spoiled the original versions by his later-period elaborations. Indeed, some of these editors of volumes of James's work today present us with the original rather than with the revised texts, though occasionally the later versions appear; it is well for the interested reader to check.

In any event, the early- and middle-period James was a prose writer of clarity and force. His language did what he wanted it to do: it precisely expressed the experience he was dealing with; the prose at once penetrated and projected that experience.

If we carefully examine a sample passage from that time we can see how effectively he wrote then. This passage is from his short novel *Daisy Miller*, and in view of what has been said before it must be noted that this quotation is from the 1879 edition, published in England a year after the first appearance of the story in a British magazine and, in America, as a book in that same year of 1878. But, as the foremost Jamesian scholar, Leon Edel, points out, James didn't have a chance to supervise the texts in either of those earlier instances; hence in his own edition in *The Complete Tales of Henry James*, Mr. Edel reprints the 1879 text. But that is still very early James, only one version and one year away from the original.

It is, of course, well known that *Daisy Miller* was the only book of Henry James's which, in his lifetime, was bought by the wide public. The passage to be examined tells of the young American, Winterbourne, on the occasion of his visit to the Colosseum by moonlight. There he is shocked to see the American girl Daisy Miller in the company of the young Italian with whom she had been going about. The Anglo-American colony had been disturbed when she was with him, without chaperonage, even in daylight, at the hour when the fashionable carriages went along the Pincian Hill. And now Winterbourne sees her at night, amid the ruins of the Flavian Amphitheater, with her questionable friend.

Behind the drama of this encounter, a great romantic tradition lies. When Winterbourne first steps into the ruins he recalls the lines about them in Byron's *Manfred*. He could have mentioned other instances; one of Goethe's letters, for example, contains a description of the Colosseum by moonlight. The same setting was used by Hawthorne in part of *The Marble Faun*. But *Manfred*, the famous lines of which Winterbourne murmurs, was the most appropriate work for him to recall, for when Manfred remembers that night in Rome, it is at the very end of the play, just before he is struck down in resisting evil spirits. And although Winterbourne, when he recites *Manfred*, has not yet seen Daisy and her companion, the passage he remembers is a thematic preparation for things to come, since Daisy herself is to die apparently as a result of the illness engendered in her by the chill air of that night. And Winterbourne, however cosmopolitan he was, probably had enough of the American puritan in him to have thought that Daisy was in the grip of an evil spirit. A passage beyond the one we are about to consider indicates that he was horrified at seeing Daisy out there that night.

Note, in another section of the passage to be quoted, how Winterbourne's flow of thought, still before he has seen Daisy, deals with the miasmatic dangers of the cool Roman nights. These were the times of the famous Roman fever (which Edith Wharton referred to, long after, in a story with that title). Winterbourne's reflections prepare us for Daisy's fatal end—though her death was possibly brought about, as much as anything else, by her country-men, including Winterbourne.

There is one other point to note about the passage to follow, a highly technical point. This is the presence of what might be termed consecutiveness. The sentences follow one another in an order of progression, leading to a climax. Henry James toward the end of his life once mentioned "my Dramatic principle, my law of successive Aspects." He was referring to plot situations, but that "law of successive Aspects" could also refer to the organic inter-connections of his sentences. In any event, this passage will demonstrate, among other things, the principle of con-secutiveness.

A week afterwards he [Winterbourne] went to dine at a beautiful villa on the Caelian Hill, and, on arriving, dismissed his hired vehicle. The evening was charming, and he promised himself the satisfaction of walking home beneath the Arch of Constantine and past the vaguely-lighted monuments of the Forum. There was a waning moon in the sky, and her radiance was not brilliant, but she was veiled in a thin cloud-curtain which seemed to diffuse and equalise it. When, on his return from the villa (it was eleven o'clock), Winterbourne approached the dusky circle of the Colosseum, it occurred to him, as a lover of the picturesque, that the interior, in the pale moonshine, would be well worth a glance. He turned aside and walked to one of the empty arches, near which, as he observed, an open carriage—one of the little Roman street-cabs —was stationed. Then he passed in among the cavernous shadows of the great structure, and emerged upon the clear and silent arena. The place had never seemed to him more impressive. One-half of the gigantic circus was in deep shade; the other was sleeping in the luminous dusk. As he stood there he began to murmur Byron's famous lines, out of *Manfred*;

but before he finished his quotation he remembered that if nocturnal meditations in the Colosseum are recommended by the poets, they are deprecated by the doctors. The historic atmosphere was there, certainly; but the historic atmosphere, scientifically considered, was no better than a villainous miasma. Winterbourne walked to the middle of the arena, to take a more general glance, intending thereafter to make a hasty retreat. The great cross in the centre was covered with shadow; it was only as he drew near it that he made it out distinctly. Then he saw that two persons were stationed upon the low steps which formed its base. One of these was a woman, seated; her companion was standing in front of her.

Presently the sound of the woman's voice came to him distinctly in the warm night-air. "Well, he looks at us as one of the old lions or tigers may have looked at the Christian martyrs!" These were the words he heard, in the familiar accent of Daisy Miller.

That mastery of prose, each sentence growing out of the one that proceeded it, is found in most of James's work, not only in the enormous mass of his fiction, but also in reminiscences, critical essays, and travel books. We shall watch it become more complicated.

The masterpiece of the earlier or middle-period James is *The Portrait of a Lady*, first published as a book in 1881. To some critics—those unable to accept James's last phase—this novel represents the crown of his achievement. It is an imposing story, carefully built, and certainly richer in fully developed characters—richer by the volume of them—than most of James's other books. But to those who prefer the so-called "major phase," the three large novels which appeared after 1900 are more excitingly profound.

Before finding our way into them, however, let us consider one of James's shorter novels (or longer stories), taking one of the masterpieces among his works in that genre. First published in 1888, and a harbinger of the excessively complicated novels to come, *The Aspern Papers* will illustrate for us the increasing technical skill of James.

Aside from the pure drama of the story—the student of Jeffrey Aspern's life who engages in a contest with the two women who have what must be a valuable collection of the poet Aspern's love letters—aside from this pure drama and its implications, the narrative contains a number of other important elements which will also appear in James's writings of his last period.

One of these elements is symbolism. At that time in France, to whose current literature James was eagerly sensitive, symbolism pervaded the literary atmosphere. James's writings became increasingly symbolistic, as the very titles of later books and stories show. Consider "The Figure in the Carpet," "The Altar of the Dead," and, of course, those last three important novels, *The Wings of the Dove*, *The Ambassadors*, and *The Golden Bowl*. Further, the content of his work became increasingly symbolistic, not in the ordinary way of using symbols, but in the very special way of the French writers of the last century, whose symbols are not designatory but rather what, taking the name from Baudelaire's famous symbolistic sonnet, "Correspondances," might be called "correspondential" symbols. In this concept, the symbols don't point toward an obvious meaning, but rather are highly suggestive. Subtle accumulations of them in a poem or story eventually suggest meanings to the responding consciousness.

In *The Aspern Papers*, one symbol of the usual literary kind has long since been observed and pointed out: Juliana Bordereau, the ancient lady to whom Aspern's letters were written many years before, wears, in what must be her nineties, "a horrible green shade over her eyes." She undoubtedly suspects from the first that the narrator, who petitions her to rent part of her Venetian palazzo to him, is questing after the Aspern Papers, and she plays a shrewd game with him, beginning by asking a fabulously high rent. That her green eyeshade makes her look like a gambler is a fairly obvious use of symbolism.

On the other hand, there are other symbolistic elements throughout the narrative which are not so easily discernible, though they prepare the reader unconsciously for important climaxes of the story. There is, for example, James's use of the human eye. This is above all appropriate, for the narrator, sneaking around the old palazzo in quest of the hidden papers, wants above all to *see*: he is after all a kind of scoptophile, a voyeur, a literary Peeping Tom. This literary sleuth is not a creative man, like Aspern, the poet of original vision; hence the narrator's fervent identification with Aspern is, among other things, ironic parody. This narrator always wants to see the eyes hidden under Juliana Bordereau's eyeshade, and finally he does see them, in a moment of dramatic intensity. This occurs when he is committing actual burglary one night in trying to find the papers, and Miss Bordereau catches him at it, fiercely calling him a "publishing scoundrel." The moment in the story is one of violent shock. As he says, "her hands were raised, she had lifted the everlasting curtain that covered half her face, and for the first, the last, the only time I beheld her extraordinary eyes. They glared at me, they made me feel horribly ashamed." James, by his adroit use of almost indiscernible symbols, has led us along to this moment of emotional explosion. And, later, the man who so badly wanted to see the Aspern Papers doesn't see them; this is the irony of his defeat.

The word *defeat* suggests the military allusions which unobtrusively though definitely occur throughout the story, also rushing together at one point to produce an important part of the action. The very name Aspern suggests war, strategy, and battles: Napoleon, overconfident and taking too many risks, sustained his first major defeat at the Austrian village of Aspern.

The narrator in James's story thinks of his search after the papers as a strategic campaign, and throughout he makes numerous (though not always readily discernible as such) references taken from the military. Like the symbol of the eyes, this military symbolism also intensifies in an important event in the story. This takes place after Miss Bordereau has died, and her ageing spinster niece—described as long, lean, and pale—has hinted to the scholar-adventurer that the papers would be his if he married her. He makes it clear to the reader that he has liked her, but to marry a woman "of such an age and such an appearance" would be unthinkable. He wanders wildly across the networks of

Venice's little canals until, toward sunset, he comes upon the enormous statue of Bartolommeo Colleoni before the Church of St. John and St. Paul. He looks up in the flaring sunset at the figure of the famous soldier of fortune astride his bronze horse. It is, he reflects, the finest of all statues of mounted figures, "unless that of Marcus Aurelius, who rides benigant before the Roman Capitol, be finer; but I was not thinking of that; I only felt myself staring at the triumphant capitain as if he had an oracle on his lips."

No—our narrator doesn't want to think of the cool stoic, Marcus Aurelius; rather, all the military symbolism which has colored his attitude makes him turn to Verrochio's horseman for a prophetic indication. Henry James knew his European history, and he would have been aware that Colleoni was famous above all for being a man of changes. Even in the period of *condittieri*, of free-lancing adventurers, Colleoni was notable for the number of times that he changed sides in the intercity wars. When our narrator returns to the palazzo to go to bed, his sleep is restless and troubled, and he wakes up in the morning prepared to make a change. Inspired by Colleoni, he will marry the unattractive woman, if he has to, in order to get the coveted papers. And then we behold the irony of his defeat, for he learns from the woman that she has burned the papers, which she assures him were of great importance.

There is much more than all this in James's long story, and many other problems to be resolved, but at least we have seen how James had learned to work out thematical matters in symbolistic terms.

But before we at last turn to the final period and all its complications, we might note that one of those complications concerns the delineation of character. James was what in those times was known as "a psychological novelist," and someone said that Henry James was a novelist who wrote like a psychologist, while his brother William was a psychologist who wrote like a novelist. This was probably intended to be more of a compliment to William than to Henry.

The so-called psychological novel first appeared in the

nineteenth century, even before the case histories of mental patients, recorded anonymously, began to turn up in the books of Richard von Krafft-Ebing and Sigmund Freud. Fyodor Dostoevsky is generally thought of, among other things, as the giant of the early psychological novel; indeed, Friedrich Nietzsche once said that all he knew about psychology he learned from Dostoevsky's novels. Dostoevsky even provided Freud, as Shakespeare did, with characters who served virtually as case studies in Freud's books on psychoanalysis.

Henry James was probably a bit too old to have learned much, if anything, from Freud, though in controversies over James's work, such as the one which has raged for many years over his story, "The Turn of the Screw," various attempts have been made to trace a Freudian influence in James.

But in these matters James was probably self-schooled more than anything else, though of course he knew his brother's books on psychology, which were quite different, however, from those of Freud. As a "psychological novelist" Henry James searched out the hidden recesses of the consciousness. The writing of novels, with or without help from Freud, had become increasingly explorative in regard to inner thoughts and feelings, especially in the case of the psychological novel. This was a pronounced advance from novel-writing in the eighteenth century, when Henry Fielding could, perhaps partly in jest, say of the hypocritical and villainous Master Blifil in *Tom Jones*—

> As he did not, however, outwardly express any such disgust, it would be an ill office in us to pay a visit to the inmost recesses of his mind, as some scandalous people search in the inmost secret affairs of their friends, and often pry into closets and cupboards, only to discover their poverty and meanness to the world.

Whether or not Fielding was trying to be ironic, or simply comic—and Freud has shown us that what we jest about we are really serious about—the point remains that earlier novels didn't go inward; fiction didn't seriously do that until the nineteenth century, particularly with Dostoevsky. At the beginning of the twentieth century we had Henry James, followed by Marcel Proust, Dorothy Richardson, James Joyce, Virginia Woolf, and William Faulkner, who didn't necessarily influence one another.

And so we go back to the later James, with a novel opening with such a clause as "She waited, Kate Croy, for her father to come in . . ."

For the thematic matter James was dealing with, that opening was what might safely be classed as perfect. As sensitive as he was to his material, he couldn't have written, "Kate Croy waited for her father to come in . . ." For he was dealing with devious people, who worked in indirection. Kate Croy in the course of *The Wings of the Dove* invents and develops a particularly vicious scheme, one of the most vicious in modern fiction. And it is all based on twisted and indirect dealings.

Even the father Kate is waiting for, in his shabby London lodging house, is a circuitous figure. A minor character in the story, he nevertheless contributes to the sinister background of Kate and her scheme. And Kate will influence Merton Densher, whom she hopes to marry, to become part of that scheme. Another principal character, Lord Mark, however unwittingly, is also a crooked, if obtuse, participant in Kate's plot.

When all these matters are considered, that beginning sentence no longer seems so odd. James in his opening words has struck off his beginning at the exact pitch: we are at once taken into a world of "shifted subjects," to use the grammatical term, and into a world of hidden parentheses, of prevalent *indirection*, where the correct order of things is reversed, slyly so.

But, set off against all the twisted and sinister manifestations in this novel, we find some straight and good people, however complicated they are in their own way. As a minor character who is notably admirable, we have the physician Sir Luke Strett. More important, there is the American heiress, Milly Theale, the "dove" of the title.

The central idea of the book is rather simple. Kate and

the man she wants to marry, Merton Densher, are poor. Densher, a journalist, makes a visit to the United States and there meets Milly Theale, an heiress. They renew their acquaintance when she goes to London. Milly is frail, with little chance to live. Kate, counting on Milly's love for Densher, forces him to pay court to the American girl; if Densher can become her husband, he will have her fortune after her death, and then he and Kate can marry comfortably. But in Venice, Lord Mark, who also wants to marry Milly, tells her of Kate's plot. Milly, whose health had been improving, turns away from life and dies. After Densher returns to London, Kate accuses him of being in love with the dead girl. When Densher learns that Milly has left him her fortune, he tells Kate he will renounce it so they can once more be as they were; but Kate leaves him forever, with the statement, "We shall never be again as we were!"

In working out the story, James of course can make it far more complex than any synopsis can indicate, giving it an intricacy which the language helps greatly to develop. And he creates some tremendous dramatic episodes besides the final one in which Kate and Densher discuss Milly's legacy, and Kate leaves him. Certainly one of the most powerful scenes in all twentieth-century fiction is the one in Venice in which Densher is turned away from Milly's door at the palazzo which goes by the ironic name of Leporelli, suggesting the name of the servant Leporello in Mozart's *Don Giovanni* who enumerates his master's love affairs.

Venice is itself a symbol, bright and cheering enough in the early days of Densher's visit there, but always suggesting the sinister in its crooked little network of dirty canals: there were similar suggestions about the background rôle of Venice itself in *The Aspern Papers*; James had based that earlier story on his knowledge that Jane Claremont, of the Shelley-Byron circle, had lived on for many years in Florence, with valuable personal papers. In resetting the story in Venice, James intensified the tale's *ambiance* of evil.

And in *The Wings of the Dove*, Venice one day turns evil for Densher. The water-city whose bright towers and porticos fare badly in a greying rain is swept by a downpour from early morning. At tea time, Densher walks across Venice in the gusts of rain; and when he arrives at the Palazzo Leporelli, he learns from one of Milly's gondoliers, in the courtyard, that Milly and her woman companion are not "receiving" that day. For the past three weeks Densher had not been among the merely receivable there, "but had taken his place for once and all among the involved and included, so that on being so flagrantly braved he recognised after a moment the propriety of a further appeal."

So he speaks with Milly's guide and superior servant, Eugenio, whom he has always regarded as a friend. On this occasion Eugenio is properly polite, but Densher is aware of some faint difference in his manner as he says that the ladies are perhaps a "leetle" fatigued. Densher observes that Eugenio doesn't give him an invitation to come back. As James writes,

> This manner, while they stood for a long minute facing each other over all they didn't say, played a part as well in the sudden jar to Densher's protected state. It was a Venice all of evil that had broken out for them alike, so they were together in their anxiety, if they really could have met on it; a Venice of cold, lashing rain from a low black sky, of wicked wind raging through narrow passages, of general arrest and interruption, with the people engaged in all the water-life huddled, stranded and wageless, bored and cynical, under archways and bridges.

It is perhaps unfair to Henry James to evoke Shakespeare at this point, because most writers, even of major stature, when compared with Shakespeare become like a cup of salt water held up to the ocean; but it must be noted that there is something in James's Venetian storm scene that suggests Shakespeare, and even if there is no violent and terrifying apostrophe to the storm, as in *King Lear*, at least in this Venetian scene we can see a relationship, such as we have in *Lear*, between Densher's inward state and the tempest. And perhaps it is not too extravagant to call up Greek tragedy, in which the chorus so often represents an extension of the problems and catastrophe confronting the doomed hero; here the people of Venice, although not definitely quoted as saying anything, provide a choral effect by their mere presence, which can hardly be construed as silent. Whether or not James was aware of any such possible comparisons, he at least partly adapted the methods of illustrious predecessors. What is more, he made those methods work; read in the full context of his novel, this storm scene is a magnificently effective piece of writing, rendered with an amplitude of power rarely found in modern novels.

There is still more to this scene. Densher "had to walk in spite of the weather, and he took his course, through crooked ways, to the Piazza, where he should have the shelter of the galleries." These are unwontedly crowded with disaffected Venetians, and tables and chairs from the outdoor caffès of the Piazza San Marco have been brought into the arcade. Its great and elegant gallery, "greasy now with salt spray," seems to Densher "more than ever like a great drawing-room, the drawing-room of Europe," but now "profaned and bewildered by some reverse of fortune." There is again the choral effect of shared and extended misery, and even a conjuring up of Venice's past with the domino masks which appear so frequently in eighteenth-century paintings of the city's activity: "He brushed shoulders with brown men whose hats askew, and the loose leaves of whose pendant jackets, made them resemble melancholy maskers"—here is again an externalization of Densher's inner problems. He has been wearing a mask at the Palazzo Leporelli.

And then Densher sees Lord Mask seated at a table in the inside part of Florian's, with a copy of the *Figaro* on his lap—Lord Mark whom, a few weeks before, Milly Theale has rejected. And at once Densher's thoughts involve Lord Mark in the immense evil of that day—

> The weather had changed, the rain was ugly, the wind wicked, the sea impossible, *because* of Lord Mark. It was because of him, *a fortiori*, that the palace was closed. Densher went round again twice, and found the visitor each time as he had found him first. Once, that is, he was staring before him; the next time he was looking over his *Figaro*, which he had

opened out. Densher didn't again stop, but he left him apparently unconscious of his passage—on another repetition of which Lord Mark had disappeared. He had spent but the day; he would be off that night; he had now gone to his hotel for arrangements. These things were as plain to Densher as if he had them in words. The obscure had cleared for him—if cleared it was; there was something he didn't see, the great thing; but he saw so round it and so close to it that this was almost as good. He had been looking at a man who had done what he had come for, and for whom, as done, it temporarily sufficed. The man had come again to see Milly, and Milly had received him. His visit would have taken place just before or just after luncheon, and it was the reason why he himself had found her door shut.

Most of this last passage borders on the stream-of-consciousness method. The sentences are, as usual in James, marked by consecutiveness, his "law of successive Aspects," but there is an almost whirling element in these sentences until, at the very end, James uses five one-syllable words, "had found her door shut," which hammer home the shock Densher has received.

There is of course a great deal of force in various aspects of this novel—psychological, thematic, moral—all interrelated and given life by the author's use of language. The psychology of evil, the evil committed every day by fairly ordinary people who can be treacherous in human relationships—the psychology of this type of behavior is expertly presented through the portraits, viewed from within, of the strong-willed Kate and the fairly weak Densher who, however, rises toward strength at the end; and there is also the evil, seen almost entirely from the outside, of the jealous meddler, Lord Mark.

Thematically, the book has several different aspects, one of the principal of which is a somewhat distorted love story. There is also greed for wealth, represented by several of the characters. And James's famous "international theme" is also present, particularly in the person of Milly Theale. The international theme in James's earlier work often showed how crafty Europeans could trick an innocent American. In James's novel *The American* (1877), a rather tough-minded man is the victim (it is interesting to note that James later considered this story somewhat implausible). In the previously mentioned *The Portrait of a Lady*, the American girl Isabel Archer is led into a trap by Europeanized Americans—and, to some extent, by her own puritan conscience. Isabel was somewhat patterned after a girl-cousin whom James had known in his youth, who had died young, of tuberculosis, a bright girl he was very fond of. Milly Theale was also modeled after her, and although Milly, like James's cousin Minny Temple, died young, Milly as a character in a novel had one advantage over Isabel Archer, who didn't die young—Milly won a victory in a way in which Isabel did not.

The moral sense was deeply important to James, and he consistently dealt with it in his work, however subtly. In *The Wings of the Dove*, Milly wins an impressive moral victory over Kate; and Densher rises toward morality as well as toward courage and strength.

In *The Ambassadors*—written before *The Wings of the Dove* but published after it—the central figure, Lambert Strether, also wins a moral victory of sorts. Like most such matters in James, the presentation of Strether's situation, and the ultimate resolution, are extremely tenuous. Again, it is the carefully refined yet always organic prose which carries the multiplex elements of the story.

One sample of the prose of this novel—indeed it is only a sentence—will give an idea of the tone of the book. But the stage must now be set for that sentence.

In the last century, American passenger ships going to England often landed at Liverpool. That James enjoyed staying there for a day or two and visiting nearby Chester, which Americans nowadays rarely see, is evident from some of his travel sketches. In *The Ambassadors*, James sends Lambert Strether to Chester after he has arrived at Liverpool, revisiting Europe after many years. Strether has a mission in Paris, symbolically an ambassadorial one, but James with his sense of consecutiveness takes him there by stages. There are two human relationships which have to be explored a little before Strether is exposed to Paris.

The sentence we are concerned with presents the medieval wall that encircles Chester, which delighted Strether; as a young man thirty years before, he had walked around the city on that wall, which now enters his fifty-five-year-old consciousness: "The tortuous wall—girdle, long since snapped, of the little swollen city, half held in place by careful civic hands—wanders in narrow file between parapets smoothed by peaceful generations, pausing here and there for a dismantled gate or a bridged gap, with rises and drops, steps up and steps down, queer twists, queer contacts, peeps into homely streets and under the brows of gables, views of cathedral tower and waterside fields, of huddled English town and ordered English country."

Few sentences in English so distinctly embody the principle of consecutiveness—again, James's "law of successive Aspects." And the sentence further illustrates this because it is not just meaningless description: early in the book it gives the reader a suggestion of the circular nature of the plot, with its continually rising and falling action, and its elaborate twisting.

One of James's technical concerns, beginning in his middle years, was the angle from which a story was told. He essentially believed in a refined and central intelligence that would properly organize and dramatize the various components of a fictional narrative. In many of his short stories and novellas, he strictly limits the point of view to that of a central character. In both *The Wings of the Dove* and *The Golden Bowl*, James occasionally changed the center of vision, letting one character control it in one section of the novel and another in another part. *The Ambassadors* focuses firmly and exclusively on the recording consciousness of Lambert Strether. James regarded that novel as artistically the most successful of all his work.

And certainly he uses Strether's consciousness to register and project some supreme effects. Strether, long a widower, expects to marry the wealthy widow, Mrs. Newsome, in the Massachusetts town where he edits a little review with her financial assistance. But before their marriage is finally arranged, she sends him to Europe to bring her son

Chad home from Paris, where he seems to be dallying
and showing no apparent interest in returning to operate
the factory (here called, in New England terminology, a
mill), which is the rather tantalizingly unnamed source of
the family's wealth. Strether meets Chad in Paris and is
soon introduced to the young Mlle. de Vionnet, with whom
Chad is presumably in love. Strether meets other friends of
Chad's, including the girl's mother, a beautiful and wordly
woman. Strether lingers in Paris, and the way in which the
city captures him is presented gradually and superbly: the
atmosphere, the tints of evening, the trees along the boulevards, the grand shuttered buildings, and above all the
luminous spirit of the place—all of these invade Strether's
consciousness, making him a helpless prisoner. No excerpts
can do justice to the skill with which James brings this
about.

When Strether doesn't return to Massachusetts, Mrs.
Newsome sends other "ambassadors," her daughter and her
daughter's husband and his sister. But Strether advises Chad
to stay on in Paris. And although he realizes that Mrs. Newsome will not marry him now, and although he has reasons
to remain in Paris, he grimly goes back to New England.
But he will always have with him, as the participating and
sympathetic reader of the book will to some extent have,
a magnificent sense of the *wonder* of Paris.

As in the case of the other major novels of James's
final phase, the action in *The Ambassadors* is mostly at the
psychological level, but once again this can lead to powerful climaxes, usually in scenes involving confrontation or
recognition. Both of these elements occur in the dramatic
high point of *The Ambassadors*, on a day when Strether
has left Paris to enjoy the French countryside.

Walking through the landscape, which reminds him of
the work of a minor French painter of the Romantic period,
Strether arranges to have dinner at an inn, and while waiting for it he sits out in a pavilion beside a river. The pro-
prietress has spoken of two other people who have ordered
dinner there and who at the moment have rowed out of
sight up the river. But soon, and to Strether it seems to pro-

vide the human touch the landscape at last needs, a man and a woman come into sight in their boat. Strether, looking at them amiably from a distance, feels the harmony between them, until suddenly he realizes that the woman has noticed him and has said something to the man, who stops rowing, so that "their course had wavered." And

> This little effect was sudden and rapid, so rapid that Strether's sense of it was separate only for an instant for a sharp start of his own. He had too within the minute taken in something, taken in that he knew the lady whose parasol, shifting as if to hide her face, made so fine a pink point in the shining scene. It was too prodigious, a chance in a million, but, if he knew the lady, the gentleman, who still presented his back and kept off, the gentleman, the coatless hero of the idyll, who had responded to her start, was, to match the marvel, none other than Chad.

In that passage, whose little touches of color seem to come from the school of impressionism—if not pointillism— Henry James shows once again how he likes to tease the reader along. And he ends his paragraph swiftly, with short words, the last of them, an enlightening monosyllable, forcibly bringing home the moment of recognition: ". . . none other than Chad."

Then, in the next line, James lets us know at once that the woman is not Mlle. de Vionnet, but Mme. de Vionnet, the mother. Strether calls out and waves to her and Chad, and they join him. After their dinner, they all return to Paris together.

Earlier, Strether would have found this liaison shocking. But his new tolerance is the result of the experience of living in Paris. And, before the book ends, Strether advises Chad to stay there and not to give up Mme. de Vionnet, although she cannot marry him because she cannot obtain a divorce from the husband from whom she has so long been separated. Strether, the failed ambassador, returns to Massachusetts alone, but with a renewed sense of life.

If *The Ambassadors* deals for the most part with Americans and Parisians in France, *The Golden Bowl* concentrates on the adventures of two Americans, one Europe-anized American, and one European, with the story taking place in England.

The rather ironically named Prince Amerigo marries Maggie Verver, the daughter of a wealthy American, Adam Verver, who has been living in England. Maggie doesn't know that her friend, Charlotte Stant, who appears for the wedding, had known the Prince before. Charlotte, brought up in Europe, was even at one time the Prince's lover; they didn't marry because neither of them had money.

Maggie, apprehensive lest her devoted father become lonely after her marriage, encourages him to marry Charlotte Stant. But the father and daughter have so close a relationship that Maggie neglects the Prince, and her father neglects Charlotte. Then Amerigo and Charlotte resume their physical relationship, which Maggie accidentally discovers after she purchases a golden bowl in a London shop. Later, the remorseful shopkeeper calls on her to confess that the bowl is cracked. The flaw is hard to see, but it had been noticed by a man several years before, who had come to the shop with a woman; it was just before Maggie's wedding, and Charlotte had been trying to find a present for her; and when Maggie realizes that Charlotte had already known the Prince at that time, she suspects their past and present relations. Maggie never accuses Charlotte directly, but with the intense intuition of these later James characters, Charlotte knows that Maggie is aware of what has been happening. Charlotte persuades her husband to take her to America, and Adam sadly goes. It is a defeat for both of them, and a triumph for Maggie, who now has the full love of her husband, as well as that of their small son.

The Golden Bowl is in many ways the most difficult of Henry James's novels to read, and if it seems more so than such books as *The Awkward Age* (1899) and *The Sacred Fount* (1901), the reason may be that *The Golden Bowl* is considerably longer than those two books. *The Awkward Age*, written soon after James's disappointment in his attempts to become a popular playwright, consists almost entirely of dialogue, while *The Sacred Fount* explores various mysterious relationships which remain unexplainable. *The Golden Bowl*, however, brings together its themes, metaphors, symbols, episodes, and psychological motivations into a comprehensible wholeness, and it achieves this unity with tremendous dramatic strength.

Like *The Wings of the Dove*, it deals profoundly with moral problems. What moral imperatives appear in *The Ambassadors* are farther up toward the surface. From a restricted New England point of view, Strether's behavior – particularly in condoning Chad Newsome's liaison – would be "immoral"; but ultimately there is no treacherous deception of an innocent human being with whom the reader is sympathetically acquainted, as in the case of the dying Milly Theale and of the originally shy and timid Maggie Verver.

In both *The Wings of the Dove* and *The Golden Bowl*, we find darker moral crimes than adultery. Adultery of course often implies deception and treachery, but not always. The complexities of life in modern civilization have caused many good-hearted human beings to ignore an ancient tribal Commandment. To say this is not to condone what can often be bad social behavior, but to comment on moral issues with which novelists often have to deal. And if we consider examples of past writers of great moral intensity, we may examine the moral system of Dante, which was based upon Aristotle's pre-Christian ethical ideas and Aquinas's interpretation of Christian ethics. In his *Inferno*, Dante put the victims of passion into the Second Circle, near the top of Hell. And although the representatives of carnal behavior whom he and Virgil found there were severely punished (Francesca da Rimini, victim of adulterous passion, is typical), they were not so hideously tormented as those in the Eighth and Ninth Circles (whom Dante met after his helicopterlike descent on the back of Geryon): in the two lower circles he found hypocrites, flatterers, and the like in the Eighth, and the traitors in the Ninth, frozen forever into the icy floor. Dante, whose Hell was essentially an imaginative projection, nevertheless drew upon eternally recurring ideas of morality for his narrative. In James—who probably didn't ever read Dante very attentively—we find larger moral problems in the instances of treachery, as in *The Wings of the Dove*, than in the mere condoning of a free life, as in *The Ambassadors*. Like Kate Croy's plot against Milly Theale, the adultery of the Prince and Charlotte is a moral crime because it involves treachery. And yet, before the end of *The Golden Bowl*, Amerigo has intimated to Maggie that he was never really too deeply involved with Charlotte.

One more point in relation to James's last major novel remains to be discussed: the technique which was the vehicle that carried all these other elements of the story—and, in the technique, particularly the language.

The characters in *The Golden Bowl* make some remarkable statements. One of the most striking of them is Prince Amerigo's comment to Maggie, near the end of the story, when he says, "Everything's terrible, *cara*, in the heart of man." And some terrible things happen in this book; Maggie, acquiring strength, *overcomes*.

Her grand scene is the one in chapter 36 when she is out at night, on the terrace and in the huge gardens of her father's country house. This is the occasion of her tense confrontation of Charlotte, who she knows will come out to her in the deep night. And when Charlotte does come out, her approach and Maggie's thoughts are given to us in one crowning sentence: "The splendid shining supple creature was out of the cage, was at large; and the question now almost grotesquely rose of whether she mightn't by some art, just where she was and before she could go further, be hemmed in and secured."

But even before this, and before the defeat of Charlotte, we have one of the most magnificent passages in all James. Out in the night, as Maggie paces back and forth, she occasionally sees the lighted smoking-room where some of the other house guests are playing bridge. She realizes her power, and how she could cry out greatly against her wrong, but in her newfound strength she doesn't do that: "Spacious and splendid, like a stage awaiting a drama, it was a scene she might people, by the press of her spring, either with serenities and decencies and dignities, or with terrors and shames and ruins, things as ugly as those formless fragments of her golden bowl she was trying so hard to pick up."

Still watching the card players, she has an intense vision of her wrong, and in her consciousness the possibility of vengeance turns itself aside.

> She might fairly, as she watched them, have missed it as a lost thing; have yearned for it, for the straight vindictive view, the rights of resentment, the rages of jealousy, the protests of passion, as for something she had been cheated of not least: a range of feeling which for many women would have meant so much, but which for *her* husband's wife, for *her* father's daughter, figured nothing nearer to experience than a wild eastern caravan, looming into view with crude colours in the sun, fierce pipes in the air, high spears against the sky, all a thrill, a natural joy to mingle with, but turning off short before it reached her and plunging into other defiles.

That is all part of a tremendous scene—and are there many such, in modern novels?

This is surely the language of a master, one who uses it organically to express an important theme and to present significant characters.

To those who like "the major phase," this scene with Maggie on the terrace is one of the supreme moments of Henry James. And remember that the first of the three novels of this period to be published began in a way which some readers might, at first acquaintance, find unpromising: "She waited, Kate Croy, for her father to come in . . ."

Index